ROUGH WEATHER SAILING

A practical guide

ROUGH WEATHER SAILING
A practical guide

by
Conrad Dixon

Ashford
Southampton
1989

Published by Ashford
1 Church Road
Shedfield
Hampshire SO3 2HW

British Library Cataloguing in Publication Data

Dixon, Conrad
  Rough weather sailing: a practical guide.
  1. Coastal waters. Rough seas. Yachts. Cruising – Manuals
  I. Title
  797.1'24

  ISBN 1-85253-158-4

Typeset by Acorn Bookwork, Salisbury, Wiltshire
Printed by Hartnolls Limited, Bodmin, Cornwall, England

Contents

List of Illustrations

INTRODUCTION

The state of the sea is what makes sailing a joy or a misery, and nowadays the science of weather forecasting is so highly developed that a really miserable bout of bad weather is avoidable. Nevertheless, there are marginal circumstances when boats will be at sea in sub-gale conditions or will experience unexpected changes in the weather that test the skills and knowledge of crews. This book is not designed for those intrepid ocean voyagers who may be faced with a West Indies hurricane, or a Bay of Bengal typhoon, but the narrow-seas or coasting cruiser, the day sailer or the inshore racer standing in the way of winds between Forces Five and Seven. In days gone by these wind forces were known, somewhat disparagingly, as "yachtsman's gales", but the truth is that with so many boats under 30 feet in length and the ferocity of tides in north-western Europe these winds raise nasty seas which require skilful boat-handling. In short, this book is all about coping with small crises during short cruises; the common currency of most yachtsmen. It was conceived as a reaction to all those meteorological books that described bad weather, but suggested no remedies, and all those seamanship books that seemed to deal only with craft laying over gently to light winds in smooth waters. Forty years of sailing in the grey-green, choppy seas of the Continental Shelf has stripped away any illusions on the latter score, and I hope that this work will help you to deal confidently with the realities of piloting your boat in safety through the occasional perils of Britain's brief summer.

Conrad Dixon
December 1988

Chapter One
READY FOR THE SEA

"When I had the Honour of writing last to Your Lordship from Rio Janeiro, I informed You that Our Ship was then ready for the Sea . . ."

Letter from John ('Foul-weather Jack') Byron
to the Earl of Egmont, 24 February 1765

Planning for hard winds and rough water can never be too thorough or too detailed, for there are no chandlers, no boatyards and no mechanics in the open sea. Rough water teases out any weaknesses in fittings and rigging, in equipment or the crew itself. This first chapter is all about those steps a prudent skipper will take before navigating his little ship offshore.

It will do no harm to start with a definition of rough weather. Waves are chiefly raised by wind, and as wind increases in strength there comes a point when the handling of the boat is dictated by sea conditions rather than the actions of the crew. Now, it is not possible to say exactly when this occurs, for a small open boat may be compelled to a certain course of action when the wind blows Force Five on the Beaufort Scale, while an ocean racer manned by a dozen or so fit young men is not hard pressed in Force Eight. This assertion itself needs instant qualification, for the heading of the craft in relation to wind direction adds its own variable. Going downwind, the open boat has less to contend with and its skipper retains control longer, while close-hauled the ocean racer is at an awkward living angle, the helming is harder and the amount of canvas set has to be reduced. Shallow water makes for steeper waves and breaking crests, whatever the wind strength; deep water for a long interval between the tops of the waves with less wind in the troughs. The weather forecasts tend to be slightly pessimistic because of the sheer size of sea areas and the necessity of painting the blackest possible picture, while in the early stages of a blow the wind can rise while the sea remains smooth. It is, therefore, an essential part of a skipper's job to know just when extra precautions need be taken. The routine preparations should have been made before the voyage began.

Routine precautions

Hatches, windows, ports, skylights and dropboards will have been closed, or so nearly closed as to allow for ventilation but deny entry to a slopping sea. The drains that empty water from the cockpit will be open, and the bilge pump or pumps will have been tested. Standing rigging has been checked for tension, and running rigging for free movement through the blocks or round the winches. The crew will know, for certain, where the hard-weather sails are stowed, and the engine will be ready for an immediate start. The battery box has a batten over it so that the batteries will not come adrift, and buoyancy aids and safety harnesses have been issued, fitted and made ready. The weather forecast has been written down, and a note made of buoyage, tidal stream changes, traffic lanes and separation areas, shallows, dangers and the times of sunset and sunrise. The echo sounder, VHF set and direction-finder will have been tested to ensure that they are in working order. Fuel tanks are comfortably full; food and water for two or three days is on board. The more detailed preparations required when rough weather is anticipated come under six headings, and these are discussed below.

Stowage

The culprits that most often cause trouble when the boat is moving over a lively sea are the cooking utensils in the galley, and tinned goods. In the former case, pans and pots need to be secured behind deep sills and wedged with towels, while tins should be out of sight in deep lockers. Books can also be fairly disabling if they jump out of shelving, and I recall encountering a freak wave off Sark in 1986 when a whole row of books leapt an 8 inch retaining bar and fell on a crewman sleeping, most properly, in the windward saloon bunk. The cure is to have an extra length of shock cord holding the *top* edge of books in position. The ready-use lockers near the galley stove should be reserved for light items – packets of cereal, dried herbs, J-cloths and bin-liners – that will do little harm if they burst out and fly across the cabin. Nowadays, many boats have small refrigerators, and it is essential to have a positive bolt or catch on the door as the standard rubber strips will not keep the unit closed in rough weather.

That takes care of the jumping articles; now for the sliders. Sleeping bags left on bunks will invariably creep to the edge and fall off; navigation instruments left on the chart table will do the same. In particular, the roller type of parallel ruler in heavy brass must always go back into a rack or case because it can do a lot of damage to shins and toes. Charts disintegrate with wet or blow away if not secured, and if your boat does not have a "downstairs" navigating position and the chart must be used in the open it is essential to protect it. The Dutch-made Combi-cover portable navigating knee-table works well in the cockpit, with courses and tidal triangles drawn by using a waterproof felt-tip pen on a plastic covering sheet. I carry the British-made Portland Plotting Board (Mark II) which is fitted with an adjustable parallel ruler and takes an Admiralty chart folded in half under similar plastic sheeting. Some items of equipment must be kept securely tied, yet near at hand. The panic bag, for example, can be tied to the cabin steps so that it keeps dry, is handy, yet may be snatched up in an emergency. (For more detail on the panic bag, see pp. 75–6 of *Grounding, Stranding and Wreck*, Ashford Press Publishing, 1988.) Torches and flares are best bracketed on a bulkhead near the cabin entrance. Wirecutters, which only come into play with a dismasting, need to be stowed low down and well out of sight.

Finally, there must be the steady propaganda barrage put out by senior members of the crew. Good stowage is a battle fought every watch, and everyone must be actively encouraged to put back that which has been taken out. Rough seas and strong winds are only agents for damage to gear and human flesh; man contributes handsomely. A sextant sat upon, a pillow on the cabin sole with a boot imprint on it, and an unbagged sail are all casualties in the stowage war, and symptoms of a careless or lazy crew.

Clothing and personal safety equipment

It is unwise to wear oilskins when near the galley stove. The worst accident I ever witnessed in forty years of sailing occurred when a crew member on a well-known racing yacht was heating-up the contents of a saucepan on the galley stove. He swayed with the roll of the ship, and as the boat moved back the other way he took an involuntary step forward and caught the hood of his oilskin jacket on the saucepan handle, bringing the boiling contents all over himself. The unfortunate victim lost all the skin from his back and had to endure skin grafting over many months. At the same time, the nearly-naked cook is also a liability. Grab rails and a belt may hold him in roughly the right position, but shoes or boots are needed in case a knife falls to the ground, while a rubber apron will deflect spilt liquid. Perhaps the best combination for a cook is short sea-boots, a rubber apron and a T-shirt with no projections to catch on anything. People off-watch should be encouraged to put their oilies to drain in an oilskin locker, strip down to underwear and get into their sleeping bags. A crew member who wedges himself, fully-clothed, into a corner when off-watch is doing nobody a service. His heat balance will be too high when he goes out on deck again; he is not properly rested and feels uncomfortable as the sweat dries inside his many layers of clothing. Sometimes, seasickness is used as an excuse for not undressing, and those who do not wish to unbuckle and stretch out may be allowed to remain in the cockpit, securely held by safety harness and out of the way. If they crave something to do – let them steer. The watch system can be adjusted so that the old hands can take an extra sleep now and be ready to take over when exhaustion compels a changeover.

It goes without saying that oilskins should be the best that money can buy, for the superior makes (such as Henri-Lloyd) may be patched at shoulder, elbow or seat and last perhaps for twenty years. Beneath, warmth is conserved by a combination of long-johns and a heavy vest with a tracksuit as the intermediate layer. On the question of boots, I am out of step with the fashionable suppliers of footwear because I do not think that the thin, ankle-hugging, tie-beneath-the knees, type of boot, so conspicuous in the advertisements, is much good at sea. What is wanted is the leak-proof, moulded, short boot, one size too large, that can be kicked off in the cabin or in the water. The yellow wellies sold as fashion accessories to jeans look well going down the pontoon or planted on footrests in bars, but after a season's use they crack and leak at the ankles; the glued joins between sole and upper part company, and they are difficult to get on and off in a pitching boat in the dark with the upper part of the body encumbered with clothing.

Buoyancy aids are commonly worn in dinghies and open boats, and safety harnesses in decked craft. Sometimes, people wear both, or have a jacket with inherent buoyancy and a built-in harness and buckle. In a decked yacht where crew go forward to raise and lower sail it is right to have a taut wire or life line linking cockpit and mainmast so that crew members may be encouraged to put on their safety harnesses down below, clip on *before* they come out into the cockpit, remain clipped-on while in the cockpit and go forward secured to the wire. It is *not* a good idea to clip on to stanchions or the wires forming the side rails between stanchions found on most yachts, or to sheets, shrouds or halyards. Safety harnesses tend to have the two types of lines shown in Fig. 1. The example on the left has a single line with two snap hooks; that on the right has two separate lines – one long and one short – with a snap hook on each end. This latter type appears to be better because of the permutations available to the user. For example, in the cockpit the short line will restrict the movement of the crew member when the boat is plunging about; on the foredeck he can secure the long

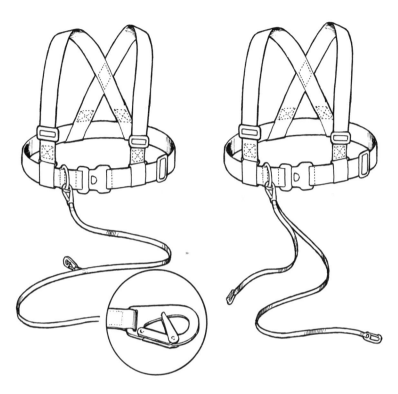

Fig. 1   Long and short harness lines

one to, say, the mast, move forward to the forestay and use the short one to clip on while lowering a headsail.

One of the problems with harnesses is that some clips tend to open themselves if they are twisted while attached to a fixed eye, and the remedy is to put a substantial rope grommet between the hook or clip and the eye. Manufacturers will claim that *their* product cannot possibly be opened in this way, but all the evidence is that a hook or clip that may be opened with the fingers will also be opened when one portion of the rounded part of the eye holds the clip and the remainder presses on the spring. In

7

Fig. 2   Rope grommet between eye and hook

Fig. 2 you can see how the intermediate grommet stops this happening. An added advantage of the grommet is that it stops that annoying clinking and rattling which so often disturbs the sleep of those off-watch and snug down below. The three main types of hooks, clips or shackles seen fitted at the extremity of harness lines are shown in Fig. 3, but it must be emphasised that the central snap shackle was not designed for this purpose and is not safe in this function.

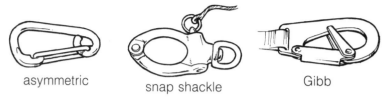

asymmetric   snap shackle   Gibb

Fig. 3   Hook types

Food and drink

A hot, soupy stew in an unbreakable metal vacuum flask is probably the best back-up nourishment when the going gets rough, and will supplement chocolate bars for energy, dry biscuits for the queasy and tonic water for salt-induced thirst. Alcohol is a no-no in these circumstances because its consumption numbs the brain, slows the limbs and accelerates the onset of hypothermia in cold weather. This interdiction does not, of course, apply once a sheltered haven is reached. Hot tea and coffee should be on tap for as long as the stove can be used, and if a vacuum flask is being prepared in advance of rocky conditions it makes sense to heat up the flask with hot water, pour it away, then fill with the beverage. That way the drink remains hot for much longer. When serving meals, remember that bowls and spoons are better than plates and knives and forks, and plan them with a view to keeping down cooking smells. Cut out frying meat and boiling vegetables; use a pressure cooker, dried onions and tinned potatoes. Grilling is almost always possible, so that bacon sandwiches made from dry or nearly dry bread and grilled bacon are a useful substitute for a full breakfast. Finally, the golden rule in yachts is that he who cooks does not wash up, so make a rota that ensures that the cook gets a few lungfuls of fresh air after his labours and somebody else toils over the sink.

Preparations on deck

Put a rag, bluetack or plasticine in the hawsepipe to keep water out, or plug it with a stopper. Turn ventilator cowls away from the expected wind direction, and lash down those items of deck gear that are going to stay up top such as boathooks, oars, fenders and spinnaker poles. Rig a lifeline running forward and have a reefing handle ready in the cockpit. White flares for warning shipping of your whereabouts and a foghorn should be near at hand; the radar reflector rigged in the "catch rain" mode and positioned at least 12 feet above sea level. Bilge pumps and their handles are often situated in the cockpit for dealing with water draining aft, but few standard production yachts have a second pump up forward to deal with

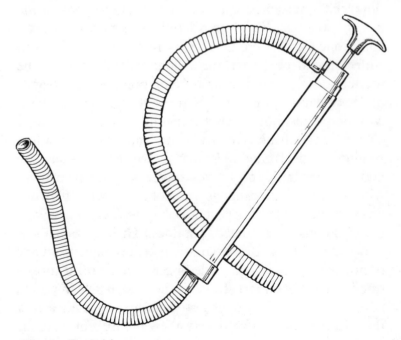

Fig. 4   Portable pump

accumulations of water in awkward spots. The solution is to carry a portable pump a little like the stirrup pumps used for putting out incendiary bomb fires in World War Two, and Fig. 4 has an illustration of the type. With one of these pumps it is possible to get at water slopping around in the forward bilge and remove it by bucket or by transfer to the lavatory pan and thence back into the sea. These plastic portable pumps are also useful for draining waste oil from sumps and drip trays and for emptying rain water from rowing dinghies. In small craft with shallow cockpits it is advantageous to have a bad-weather tiller extension of the type used in racing dinghies. They confer greater leverage to the helmsman, and there is the added benefit that he can keep up to the forward end of the cockpit and be sheltered from wind and spray.

Personal readiness

The reaction of the body to stress induced by the onset of rough weather begins with the release of adrenalin so that the heart rate and blood pressure rise, the liver releases more sugar into the blood and the blood vessels contract to reduce heat loss. After about half an hour these adaptive responses weaken in effect and there is a slow relapse into apathy. The skipper, navigator and helmsman are less likely to become apathetic at the same rate because they have functions to perform, but those crew members who are usually active on deck have much less to do in unsettled conditions once the sail changes have been made. These sail changes may take up the whole half-hour of adrenalin release so that the loss of interest in what is going on coincides with less work for mind and body. Drowsiness, apathy and nausea are often stages on the road to seasickness, with sensitivity to diesel fumes, tobacco or cooking smells a powerful warning signal. In some cases, the individual is able to keep his face to the wind, breathe deeply and face it out. In others, the chemical solution should have been tried *before* the need became evident. Anti-seasickness tablets are best used in two stages. The Royal Navy, for example, supplies Kwick Kwells (hyoscine hydrobromide) in 0.3 milligram tablet form, and recommends that the best regime is to start with one or two tablets about an hour before exposure to unusual motion and repeat the dose about every six hours. A potential sufferer should not consume more than six tablets in twenty-four hours. The celebrated mountaineer and yachtsman Bill Tilman, who made many adventurous voyages in old wooden Bristol Channel pilot cutters, swore by Dramamine which has to be taken the night before sailing. Scopoderm TTS is the "magic patch behind the ear" which is reputed to be truly magical but, at the time of writing, requires the production of a medical certificate. My own cure is free and does not involve any bureaucracy. A half-pint of clean sea-water, downed in one, nearly always does the trick.

The personal gear carried by everyone on board should include gloves and a knife with a spike. Matches and smoking materials need to be in polythene bags or water-proof tobacco pouches, and those who wear glasses may wish to tie string to the side struts and loop it round the back of the neck to avoid parting company with them. The skipper and navigator are going to be peering at charts at intervals, and if they can bear the derision that invariably follows the production of a monocle may find one invaluable. Glasses fall off when the head is down over the chart table, but a monocle clenched between cheekbone and eyebrow stays wedged in place. Similarly, there is nothing sissy in using a chart magnifier for reading the small print in volumes of sailing directions, or getting out the binoculars to check the characteristics of a buoy or lighthouse. At night, a small pocket torch will be useful when trimming or tweaking, working the winches or reading the log, and its dim illumination will not blind the helmsman as he concentrates on the compass card and his course.

Personal preparedness for boisterous conditions at sea rests on a strong psychological basis, and the skipper is the man who can create an atmosphere of calm and wisdom by keeping everyone informed and by indicating through his confident attitude that a tumbling sea is a normal part of any cruise and that there are standard and well-tested ways of coping with the situation. He should combine order and consensus, and arrive at decisions in an open way. He must explain what is going on, how he proposes to deal with it, and what each individual will do. He should say, for example, what sail combination is about to be employed, and why. He will say who will perform the various functions, and when. He will indicate the tactics to be used at certain stages of the voyage, but will be prepared to modify them if experienced crew members have local knowledge or previous experience in the area. Someone may know that one harbour nearby is easier to get into than another; that there is a dangerous bar to be got over at a certain state of the tide, or that anchorage behind one particular headland gives a better night of rest than another. As so often in sailing, he may have to decide that the longest way round is the safest way there, and tell everybody so. Duties may have to be swapped round, and there may be time for a meal and hot drink *before* hard winds make life difficult. The thing to avoid is raised voices and red faces, for a calm and decisive demeanour on the part of the skipper and perfect

13

knowledge among the crew will enable everyone to face up to the problem and overcome it as a team, not as frightened individuals.

Emergencies

An emergency is just another name for a new priority, for while the overall object may be to get the boat safely to its destination, a leak in the loo inlet hose means that steps must be taken urgently to keep the boat afloat while the overall object is achieved. Leaks apart, the three major emergencies likely to be encountered are dismasting, fire and man overboard. Of the first, there is not much to be said. When a mast goes by the board the principal danger is that the floating spar and boom will knock a hole in the hull, and it is chiefly a matter of using the wirecutters speedily and effectively to sever the remaining shrouds. If there is a chance of saving the spars, leave one wire attached – preferably the backstay – for towing them home. If the sea is rough – let 'em go!

Fires on boats have two main causes – the cooker and the engine – and extinguishers should be bracketed close to each potential hazard. A third extinguisher may be stored forward in a hanging locker or wardrobe, and the reason for having it there is that a flare-up in the near vicinity of the cooker or engine often prevents you getting to its appointed extinguisher, and it makes sense to have a spare well removed from the potential seat of a fire. My experience is that the small 682 gram aerosol types made for motor vehicles are better value than the massive jobs sold in chandlers, while the smothering fire blanket will, nine times out of ten, put out a small blaze in its early stages when the denial of air is enough to check combustion. Most boat fires are easily prevented, and I would suggest that they are rare on craft where the crew are trained to switch off cooking gas at the cylinder after *every* meal, and where regular pumping out of the bilges prevents the accumulation of inflammable gases in the bottom of the boat. The owner who secures his gas bottles in a well-ventilated locker with rope or shock cord, and who keeps his engine spotlessly clean and free from fuel drips, is also greatly reducing the likelihood of fire.

There are no hard and fast rules in the late 1980s for recovering a man in the water, but a drill must be prepared and rehearsed to meet most contingencies. I use the mnemonic TESSIE O'SHEA IS LOOKING FOR LIKELY LADS, which stands for TURN, SHOUT, LIFEBUOY, LOOKOUT and LEE SIDE. As the object is to make a quick recovery and thus keep as close as possible to the man in the water, I believe that former theories based on a figure-of-eight manoeuvre or circling back for a pick-up are now out of date and the quick-stop technique is best. No matter the point of sailing, or what canvas is spread, the first thing to do is to turn, or tack, so as to achieve a hove-to position, as near dead in the water as may be. Shout is self-explanatory, as is lifebuoy. One lifebuoy may not be enough, and after the usual horseshoe-shaped buoy has gone over the side I would add a dan-buoy, fenders, cockpit cushions, or anything that will float and give a line of objects back to the casualty. Lookout means that one person will be told to do nothing else but keep an eye on the man in the water, pointing if necessary at all times to where he was last seen. Lee side is a little ambiguous, but my preference is for a drift down from up-wind so that the man in the water is on the boat's lee side. Recovery is often the hardest part of the operation, for I have never had any luck trying to drop the belly of the mainsail to use as a stretcher or employing the boom, topping lift and main sheet as an improvised crane. In practice, it seems that the best way of getting the casualty on board in a hurry is to wrap the line from the horseshoe lifebuoy round and round him, and fasten lassoes made from mooring warps around trunk and arms and legs so that the poor devil ends up Gulliver-like in a cocoon of rope and is hauled in unceremoniously through the guardrails. When practising, please do not use a human being, even on the finest day, but make do with a facsimile constructed from fenders and an old boiler suit. Time your trial, and if it takes longer than twenty minutes find ways of speeding the recovery process.

One last word about equipment and treatment of the casualty. A boarding ladder or a folding side ladder come in useful when getting a man out of the water, and a half-inflated rubber dinghy is ideal for rolling him into at the first stage of recovery. Nowadays, man overboard justifies the transmission of a MAYDAY by VHF, and the co-operation of other craft will be vital if a square search has to be carried out. The treatment of a crew member who has been in the sea for even a few minutes must be based on the assumption that he is, at the very least, severely chilled. If he is shivering, put him in a warm place, cover him with sleeping bags, and give him as much warm tea as he will drink. Do not allow him alcohol or tobacco at this stage. I will have more to say about treatment for hypothermia and other conditions and injuries in Chapter Seven which covers all the aspects of first aid in small craft.

Chapter Two
THE RESTLESS WAVE

Eternal Father, strong to save,
Whose arm doth bind the restless wave,
Who bidd'st the mighty ocean deep
Its own appointed limits keep:
O hear us when we cry to thee
For those in peril on the sea.

W. Whiting, 1825–78

Wind makes waves, and wind is experienced when there
are differences in atmospheric pressure at various places
on the surface of the earth, with low-pressure areas acting
as shallow holes which become less deep as air pours into
them. High-pressure areas are gentle mounds which shed
air as part of an automatic levelling process. This simple
version of events needs the addition of three other factors:
temperature, the earth's rotation and wind direction.

Temperature has a part to play in creating wind, as
when the sun-heated land sucks in air from the cooler
sea. In Fig. 5 you may see both aspects of the land and
sea breeze effect with, on the left, the sea breeze blowing
onshore as the sun rises in the heavens; on the right, the
land breeze blows offshore at night as the sea is warmer
and the cooler land air flows seawards.

The rotation of the earth imparts a twist to the ultimate
direction of wind with the *Coriolis Force* deflecting air
masses to the right in the northern hemisphere and to the
left in the southern. As a result, the wind flows in a
clockwise direction around and away from a northern
hemisphere high-pressure area and flows into and counter-

17

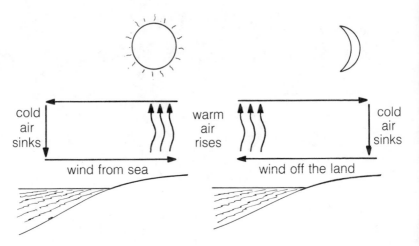

cold
air
sinks

wind from sea

warm
air
rises

wind off the land

cold
air
sinks

Fig. 5   Land and sea breezes

clockwise around a low-pressure area. This latter phenom-
enon may be seen in Fig. 6 where the wind is at an angle
of about 30° to the isobars outlining part of a depression
crossing the British Isles.

The general direction of the wind throughout the year
is influenced by where you happen to be on the surface of
the earth, and in northern Europe – part of the temperate
zone – there is tendency towards low pressure and
westerly winds. However, in the summer when most
sailing for pleasure takes place, there are two distinct
influences on the weather. The anticyclone that hovers,
almost permanently, over the Azores spills over to spread
over western Europe, and there is virtually uniform
pressure over the British Isles, western and northern
France and Spain. Warm, dry weather ensues with light
easterly winds influenced by the land and sea breezes
pattern. Between May and July this type of weather
sometimes alternates with fairly mild disturbances as the
ridge of high pressure is broken down and reforms. The

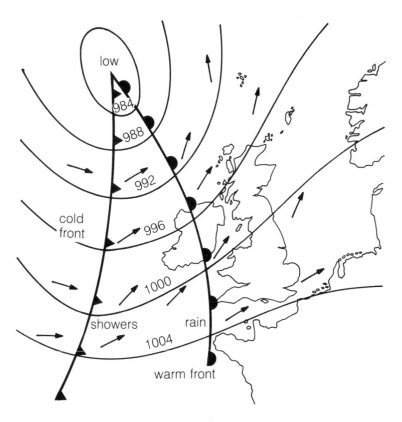

Fig. 6   Typical wind directions in a depression

disturbed westerly air stream – often in trough or col form – is driven north and dispersed as high pressure re-asserts itself with the 1015 isobar (considered by many to be the frontier post between good and bad weather) moving up into Scandinavia.

From the foregoing you will have gathered that, in general, high pressure is associated with less wind and low pressure with more wind; that wind occurs when air flows from high to low, and that what concerns yachtsmen

19

most is how fast this exchange takes place and what alterations in wind direction may be anticipated. The speed of the wind is directly related to the pressure gradient, which is represented on weather maps by the spacing of the isobars. These maps are constructed from data collected from a variety of sources. The Meteorological Office collates the data, makes synoptic charts by drawing in the isobars, and issues forecasts. The spacing of the isobars is what counts, for the rough rule is the closer the isobars the steeper the gradient and the stronger the wind. For example, on those rare occasions when the isobars are about 100 kilometres (say 55 miles) apart the wind is likely to be blowing at about 100 kilometres an hour, or Force Ten on the Beaufort Scale.

Naturally, most of the weather information we are going to need comes easily enough by radio, fax machine or telephone call, but when these mechanical aids are not available, or when sailing in waters beyond radio range, or when abroad and having an imperfect grasp of the language, you may have to read your own weather and work out your own forecast. Let us see what can be done in a self-help situation.

Buys-Ballot's law

No instruments are required to find out where the predominant area of low pressure may be, for the wise old Dutchman, Buys-Ballot, discovered about a century and a half ago that if you stand facing the wind with your arms outstretched in the northern hemisphere the area of low pressure will be about where your right hand is pointing. This information can be particularly useful if the yacht is in a high-pressure area during the summer months, for the direction indicated by the pointing hand is quite often the approximate direction of wind for tomorrow morning.

Barometers and barographs

A single reading from an instrument gives general information, but it is the rate of change, or tendency, that tells you in a short period of observation of, say, three hours, what is going to happen. The two sorts of barometers both measure atmospheric pressure, but in different ways.

The mercurial barometer, invented by Torricelli in 1643, is a glass tube filled with mercury and then inverted in a cistern containing more mercury. The mercury in the tube falls at first to leave a vacuum in the top, and then the level in the tube varies as air pressure acts on the surface of the mercury in the cistern. The aneroid barometer, perfected by Lucien Vidie in 1843, is a thin metal box, partially exhausted of air and then hermetically sealed. Variations in the atmospheric pressure cause the ends of the box to flex in and out, and this movement is conveyed by levers and springs to a moving hand on the dial of the instrument which tells you what the prevailing pressure may be.

Barographs contain a series of partial vacuum boxes which operate levers and convey movement to a pen which makes an ink trace on a chart. Few yachts carry mercurial barometers because they take up a lot of space and have to be mounted on gimbals, so that the aneroid barometer or the barograph – as shown in Fig. 7 – are most commonly employed to give information on the actual and relative air pressures.

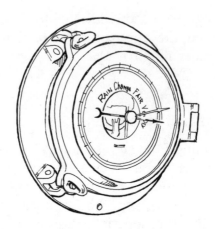

bulkhead-mounted aneroid barometer

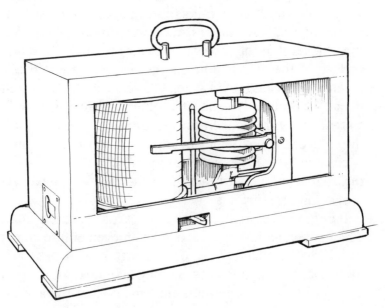

Fisher 207M barograph

Fig. 7   Aneroid barometer and barograph

Anenometer

The standard height for positioning an anenometer is 10 metres or 33 feet, and that is why you see so many of them mounted at the top of masts. They are useful in determining the strength of wind when the boat is stationary, but it will be appreciated that when the craft is moving up- or down-wind there has to be an addition or subtraction for the speed of the yacht.

Additionally, they are notoriously prone to exaggerating the force of the wind. I noted this exaggeration during a routine Channel crossing from Cherbourg to Portsmouth in August 1988. My ketch, the *Waveney Harrier*, had a Force Six wind on the beam, a figure confirmed by a current weather report from the Channel Light Vessel. A sloop voyaging in company about a mile away was recording 30 knots – the mid-point of Force Seven – on her anenometer from time to time. It seems that the whipping action of the mast as the sloop breasted the waves may have contributed to this high reading, while gusts tended to confer a lagging effect on the instrument by giving a wind strength higher than the true wind for quite long periods. Anenometers may deceive, and the reading should be treated in the same way as a log reading for water speed which shows an acceleration when a boat is surfing down-wave. Readings for logs and anenometers should be *averaged* to give the right picture.

Understanding the relative changes in pressure

Generally speaking, the rate of fall in pressure in a three-hour period is a valuable indicator of worsening weather.

A fall of 2 or 3 millibars is an alarm signal; a fall of 5 millibars or more is a warning of rapid deterioration.

This latter process has three stages. First, the rapid fall is noted as the black pointer on the aneroid barometer moves swiftly away from the moveable red pointer. Second, the figure displayed equals, or goes lower than, that given at the centre of the nearest depression or low mentioned in the last forecast. Finally, the wind remains about the same as before, thus signalling that the centre of the low is still a long way off.

A slow fall in pressure in the summer months, when temperatures are high, often presages outbreaks of thundery rain and, if the fall continues for, say, twenty-four hours, the indications are that the approaching unsettled spell will go on for some time. Continuing high pressure, on the other hand, means that calms and light breezes will alternate, with the land and sea breeze effect (shown in Fig. 5) giving a pattern to the day. The sea breeze will start at mid-morning and reach its best speed by mid-afternoon. The land breeze starts in the early hours of the morning and is strongest about breakfast time. Between 0800–1000 and 1900–2100 calms may be expected. A rapid rise in the barometer reading accompanied by a veering (clockwise-shifting) wind *sometimes* means the onset of bad weather, but only in about one in three instances. The effect of wind on the surface of the sea may be seen in Fig. 8 where in the third, fourth and sixth columns the exact correlation is set out.

The Beaufort wind scale

Sir Francis Beaufort, Hydrographer of the Navy for twenty-six years, perfected the first version of the wind scale that bears his name in 1806 when he was serving in HMS *Woolwich*. Officially adopted by the Admiralty for all naval ships in 1838, the wind scale has been much modified, up-dated and re-interpreted by meteorologists and writers on maritime subjects since then as the effect of winds on fishing smacks and square-rigged ships has been translated into their impact on sailing yachts and motor vessels. For example, in the original Beaufort notation it was said that in Force Three – a gentle breeze – a "well-conditioned Man-of-war under all sail and clear full would go three to four knots in smooth water". A fast cruising sloop with a big genoa or spinnaker set might go at twice that speed nowadays. In looking at Fig. 8 (pp. 26–7), do not forget column 5. It has the land criteria, and may be useful when leaving home to go down to the boat for the weekend having missed the shipping forecast.

Wave action in the open sea

Contrary to what you might think, waves do not move very far, and the best simile for their progression is to think of the movement of a rolling pin under a silk rug. Wave action in a rough sea is depicted in Fig. 9 where the pattern of movement is essentially circular and cyclical so that while the water at the crest is going one way the water particles in the trough are moving the other. This does much to explain the staggering motion of a boat moving in the direction of a running sea which surges on the crest and slows in the trough. In deep water this latter effect may be more pronounced as the sails are blanketed by the crests when the hull is in the troughs. Going against the run of the waves, a boat will make brief headway in the troughs and be thrown back on the crests.

Force	Description	Speed in knots	Height of waves in feet (open sea)	Conditions on land	Conditions at sea
0	Calm	less than 1	–	Calm; smoke rises vertically	Sea like a mirror
1	Light air	1–3	0.5	Direction of wind shown by smoke drift, but not by wind vanes	Ripples with the appearance of scales are formed but without foam crests
2	Light breeze	4–6	0.5	Wind felt on face; leaves rustle; ordinary vane moved by wind	Small wavelets, still short but more pronounced; crests have a glassy appearance and do not break
3	Gentle breeze	7–10	2	Leaves and small twigs in constant motion; wind extends light flag	Large wavelets; crests begin to break; foam of glassy appearance; perhaps scattered white horses
4	Moderate breeze	11–16	3.5	Raises dust and loose paper; small branches are moved	Small waves, becoming longer; fairly frequent horses
5	Fresh breeze	17–21	6	Small trees in leaf begin to sway; crested wavelets form on inland waters	Moderate waves, taking a more pronounced long form; many white horses are formed (chance of some spray)
6	Strong breeze	22–27	9.5	Large branches in motion; whistling heard in telegraph wires; umbrellas used with difficulty	Large waves begin to form; the white foam crests are more extensive everywhere (probably some spray)

7	Moderate gale	28–33	13.5	Whole trees in motion; inconvenience felt when walking against wind	Sea heaps up and white foam from breaking waves begins to be blown in streaks along the direction of the wind
8	Fresh gale	34–40	18	Breaks twigs off trees; generally impedes progress	Moderately high waves of greater length; edges of crests begin to break into spindrift; foam is blown in well-marked streaks along the direction of the wind
9	Strong gale	41–47	23	Slight structural damage occurs (chimney pots and slates removed)	High waves; dense streaks of foam along the direction of the wind; crests of waves begin to topple, tumble and roll over; spray may affect visibility
10	Whole gale	48–55	29	Seldom experienced inland; trees uprooted; considerable structural damage occurs	Very high waves with long overhanging crests. The resulting foam in great patches is blown in dense white streaks along the direction of the wind. On the whole the surface of the sea takes a white appearance. The tumbling of the sea becomes heavy and shocklike. Visibility affected
11	Storm	56–63	37	Very rarely experienced; accompanied by wide-spread damage	Exceptionally high waves (small and medium-sized ships might for a time be lost to view behind the waves). The sea is completely covered with long white patches of foam lying along the direction of the wind. Everywhere the edges of the wave crests are blown into froth. Visibility affected
12	Hurricane	more than 64	–	–	The air is filled with foam and spray; sea completely white with driving spray; visibility very seriously affected

Fig. 8   The Beaufort wind scale

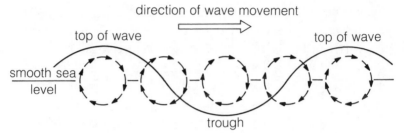

Fig. 9 Wave action: surge on the crests; slowed in the troughs

Measurement of waves

Waves can be measured, and thus classified, by reference to their length, height and period. The process is shown graphically in Fig. 10 where length is the distance between two successive crests, and height the vertical distance between a line joining two crests and the trough. The period is the time in seconds taken by successive crests to pass fixed points, such as the wave posts often seen on the coast of Holland. The height of waves is often over-estimated, and in the waters of the Continental Shelf

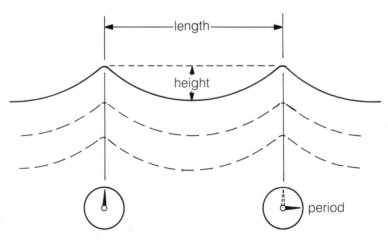

Fig. 10 Measurement of a wave

rarely exceeds 18 feet. The best-documented wave height is the 80-footer observed from the *Empress of France* in the North Atlantic in 1926. The fact that this colossal sea did damage 65 feet above the waterline seems to substantiate its height and ferocity. Observations of this kind from a moving ship carry more weight than reports from land stations or lighthouses where wind may carry heavy spume or spray great distances and waves may lick up a standing structure to give a false impression of enormous height.

The formation of swell

Swell is an old pattern of waves that are no longer directly driven by wind, and the individual waves of a swell slowly diminish in height with time as their period and length increases. When swell gets into water that has a depth of less than half of its length it begins to interact with the sea bed. The length decreases, but the period remains the same, and the height increases. It has been calculated that when a low swell, having a ten-second period and a height of 2 feet, reaches a depth of 5 feet the height increases dramatically to 3 feet, and a wave breaks. Breaking waves are of two types. Some merely spill over

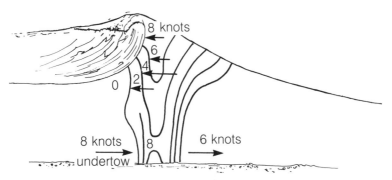

Fig. 11   A breaking wave in shallow water

into a frothy mass and do little harm: others, as in Fig. 11, topple over and acquire considerable momentum at the point where the breaking crest crashes down onto the "smooth" left by the previous wave.

Wave motion in the shallows

The shoal water effect noted above works in much the same way with wind-driven waves, and confers one positive advantage in that the position of rocks or shoals that do not normally appear above a calm surface will be revealed by a breaking wave. A wind-driven wave will usually break when the ratio between depth and length is about 1 : 10. The steepness of a wave also plays a part, because when a wave achieves a height ratio of 1 : 13 with the length it will break whatever the depth of water. From the yachtsman's point of view the chief danger arising from breaking waves in shallow water comes when approaching harbour. Some walled harbours, and Zeebrugge is an example, are so massive that reflected waves cause a rough sea in the offing. These waves rebound from large harbour works in the manner of a snooker ball bouncing from a cushion, and if the original wave was at a wide angle to the wall the ensuing cross-sea makes for very disturbed water. Of course, if the wave strikes square on to the wall or mole a massive standing wave is formed which will embarrass any craft that gets too close. The moral is that when making for a walled harbour in rough weather it is best to come up to the entrance so that you can "see down the throat" rather than sidling in parallel to breakwaters or piers.

"Fetch"

The height of waves is much influenced by the "fetch" of the wind, the unimpeded distance it has blown over open sea. As may be seen in Fig. 12, the waves get higher the greater the "fetch" or distance from the cliffs. I want to end this chapter by giving some statistics about the influence of time and distance on wave heights, lengths and periods, and relate the information to Beaufort Scale winds of Forces Five, Six and Seven.

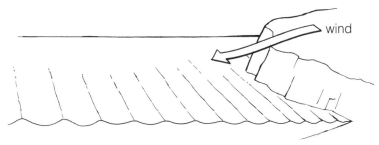

Fig. 12 "Fetch". The waves grow higher as the wind blows longer over the open sea

Behaviour of waves over time

The purport of Fig. 13 is to show that the longer the wind blows the higher and longer are the waves.

Duration of blow in hours		6	12	24	48
Wind Force Five	Height in feet	3½	4½	5½	7
	Length in feet	140	180	280	380
	Period in seconds	5	6	7½	8½
Wind Force Six	Height in feet	5	6	8	10
	Length in feet	180	270	360	530
	Period in seconds	6	7	8½	10
Wind Force Seven	Height in feet	7	8	11	14
	Length in feet	250	360	520	730
	Period in seconds	7	8½	10	12

Fig. 13 Behaviour of waves over time

31

Behaviour of waves over distance

The influence of "fetch" on wave characteristics is shown in Fig. 14: the greater the "fetch" the higher and longer the waves.

"Fetch" in miles		50	100	200	500
Wind Force Five	Height in feet	3½	4½	5½	7
	Length in feet	120	180	250	360
	Period in seconds	5	6	7	8½
Wind Force Six	Height in feet	5	6	7	9
	Length in feet	140	250	320	450
	Period in seconds	5	7	8	9½
Wind Force Seven	Height in feet	7	8	10	12
	Length in feet	180	330	400	500
	Period in seconds	6	8	9	10

Fig. 14   Behaviour of waves over distance

A last word about waves

The underlying purpose of this analysis of wave heights, lengths and periods is to assure readers that in the North Sea and English Channel, during summer, the chances of meeting very high waves are negligible.

However, height is not everything, and elsewhere some very nasty 5-footers may be encountered in, say, the Ijselmeer where shallow water and high winds create "pinnacle" seas that wet the mainsail up to the crosstrees and make for a bumpy ride. Similarly, quite moderate seas will become fiends off headlands when they tangle with a tidal race, as in the cases of Portland, St Albans and Alderney. The effect of swell can be devastating on windless days when waves roll in from a decayed disturbance, or signal wind at a distance, and the bad places are the west coast of Ireland, the Sole Bank in the Western Approaches, the north coast of Devon and Cornwall between Hartland Point and Lands End and the north Brittany coast west of Les Sept Iles. "Fetch" and a long blow keep waves high and, although the shoal water affect may sometimes make things rougher under the land, the yachtsman will always seek the wind shadow the land provides and where the restless wave is put to sleep.

Chapter Three
STORIES OF WINDS

"The seaman tells stories of winds, the ploughman of bulls; the soldier details his wounds, the shepherd his sheep."

Sextus Propertius, an elegiac
poet of the first century B.C.

Weather lore

In an age dominated by scientific methods of seeking out the truth there is a tendency to be sniffy about weather lore, but as we all have, despite ourselves, great swatches of it in the attics of our minds it will be helpful to go through the sayings to see which ones may have some scientific basis and thus provide a kind of shorthand for reading the weather. The classic: "Rain afore seven, Fine afore eleven," draws attention to the fact that there are limits to the amount of rainfall produced by fronts associated with eastward-moving low-pressure systems, and that if it has been raining during the night the odds are that there will be an improvement by mid-day. In the best meteorological tradition, of course, the anonymous compiler hedged his bet and added: "Rain arter eleven, Rain all day."

Some lore is of great antiquity. The traditional rhyme dealing with red skies at morning and evening seems to derive from Chapter 16 of St Matthew's Gospel, while in *Henry VI*, William Shakespeare points out the benign effect of cumulus by emphasising that: "Every cloud engenders not a storm."

A weather change is often preceded by the appearance of a halo around the sun or moon, and the more distant the halo from the heavenly body the nearer at hand the coming rain. Hence the fishermen will say to each other: "Far halo, near rain," and then look for the open side of the halo to see where the wind will come from. Weather lore is not just the property of the ill-educated, for it was Admiral Robert FitzRoy, a descendant of Charles II and commander of the *Beagle* that carried Charles Darwin on an epic voyage of discovery, who coined the line: "Before a storm the sea heaves and sighs," to illustrate the point made in the last chapter that swell is often a sign of wind at a distance.

Some of the most useful sayings are those that link weather signs to sail changes, and an example is: "Mackerel sky and mare's tails, Make lofty ships carry low sails." This signifies that thickening cirrus and fast-moving cirro-cumulus clouds turning to cirro-stratus are indications of unsettled weather about 500 miles away. Another version coming somewhat later in the process is: "If clouds are gathering thick and fast, Keep sharp lookout for sail and mast," while the skipper or navigator will be looking at the barometer and recalling that old saw: "When the glass falls low, Prepare for a blow."

These doggerel verses are describing the near approach of a depression, and it is time to turn towards the scientific explanation and look at the causes of the depressions that so often cross the British Isles.

Depressions

Typically, a mass of warm tropical air moves around the edges of the Azores High and makes its way north-eastward. A mass of cold Polar air moves around the edges of the Iceland Low and starts moving south-westwards. They meet on the Newfoundland Banks and, because the two air masses are reluctant to mix, the warm air rises – as shown in Fig. 15(a). The line of separation between the air masses is called the frontal surface. In the course of time the faster-moving cold air back-fills to create the profile shown in Fig. 15(b) with a leading warm front and trailing cold front. Fig. 15(c) shows the folding of the cold air around a warm wedge pivoted on a focus of low pressure.

For the next stage we have to refer back to Fig. 6. The warm front has heavy rain at its leading edge, as shown by the rounded modules fringing the thick right-hand line, while the cold front has showers, shown by the triangles on the left-hand thick line. The wind is blowing anticlockwise and at an angle of about 30° to the isobars. The yachtsman in the cockpit sees the physical manifest-ations. He observes the thickening clouds and notes the falling barometer. The clouds close in, and it feels muggy. Rain begins to fall, and the wind increases in strength. Between the fronts there is a drop in temperature, the wind veers more westerly, or even north-westerly, and there follows a series of hard squalls. Slowly, the rain begins to slacken and the clouds lighten. Patches of blue sky appear, and a pattern of cumulus clouds is established as pressure slowly rises. Generally, when the depression is part of a family, there will be a respite of between six and twelve hours before the next hard blow. The centres of most depressions pass north of the British Isles, but when this is not the case the shape of the land steers them up the Bristol or the English Channel. In the latter case, the Straits of Dover have a funnelling and compressing effect so that the worst weather will be experienced in the southern North Sea.

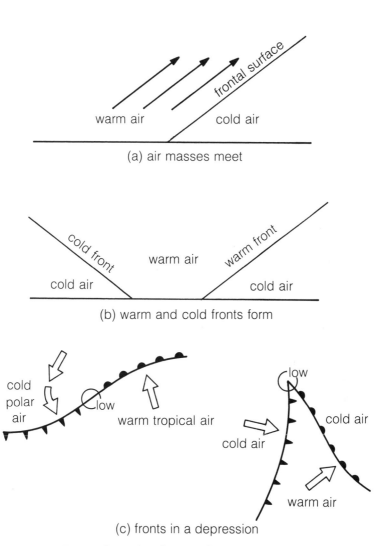

(a) air masses meet

(b) warm and cold fronts form

(c) fronts in a depression

Fig. 15   Formation of a depression

Mastering a depression

Given their predictable nature, is there any way of mastering depressions? Sometimes, progress may be accomplished against the line of depressions spilling out of the Atlantic, but only when they are small and regular in nature (the process is outlined in Fig. 16). A yacht, coming down from the Essex coast to round North Foreland, receives a forecast to the effect that a shallow depression is about to pass through the Straits of Dover. As it happens, the tide has gone foul and four hours at anchor will be as advantageous as plugging into foul wind *and* tide together. The skipper draws his weather chart (in a manner shortly to be described) and sees that there will be a window of opportunity at about the time of the next forecast. He goes inshore to anchor in the Small Downs in sight of the golf club at Sandwich, and the crew have a restful caulk off the land all afternoon. At 1800 he has the new forecast, which tells of a reasonable night with the wind round in the north-west and the shore giving shelter. In four hours the depression has blown through, the wind has turned favourable; the tide ditto. Congratulating himself on his low cunning, the skipper gets in his anchor and prepares for a run down to

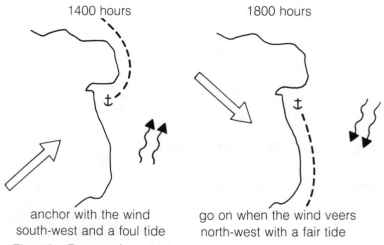

anchor with the wind
south-west and a foul tide

go on when the wind veers
north-west with a fair tide

Fig. 16   Depression strategy

Brighton or Newhaven before the next depression comes through.

Weather forecasts by radio

The four "bankers", as it were, are the BBC shipping forecasts broadcast on Radio Four (1515 metres or 198 kilohertz) at 0033, 0555, 1355 and 1750 daily. Supplements are the BBC inshore waters forecasts on Radio Four at 0038, and on Radio Three (247 metres or 1215 kilohertz) at 0655. These forecasts can be picked up with a transistor radio by vessels close to the British Isles, but for the next type of forecast you will need a VHF set. Coastal radio stations broadcast weather bulletins twice a day in the morning and evening. In 1988, there were thirty-six such stations spaced between Lands End and Wick, Jersey and the Hebrides. They are listed in *Reed's Nautical Almanac* with times of transmission, working frequencies, channels and areas covered.

If you should happen to miss all the morning forecasts it is perfectly proper to call up the nearest coastal radio station and ask for a twenty-four hour forecast for the sea areas you will be sailing across. In case of urgency, but *not* as a matter of routine, you can make the same kind of call to the Coastguard on Channel 16 VHF.

Weather forecasts by telephone

A limited number of meteorological offices will give reports of present and local weather, and they are listed in *Reed's Nautical Almanac*, but British Telecom's Marinecall telephone service was devised to cope with the majority of callers. Marinecall forecasts are updated three times a day during the summer months and group weather

39

RING 0898 500, THEN:

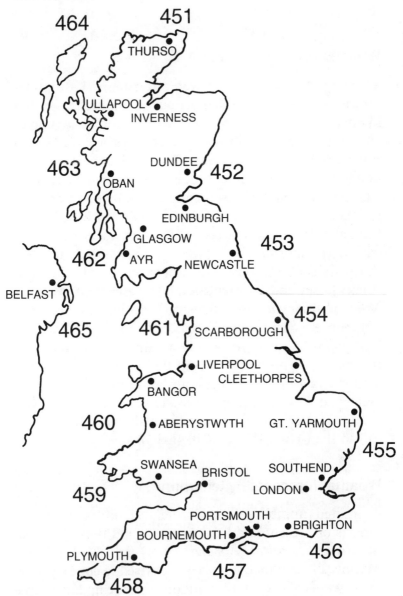

Fig. 17 The Marinecall areas and numbers

details in three sections. First, you get the recorded forecast for a strip about 12 miles wide on the British coast; then, where appropriate, a similar report for the other side – the Cherbourg peninsula or the Irish coast. As the recording goes on it deals with temperatures, times of high water and sea states, ending with a long-term prognosis. As may be seen from Fig. 17, the initial dialling figures are 0898 500 followed by a three-figure number for your sea area. Fig. 17 is a larger version of the Marinecall card supplied free (ring 01 236 3500 to get one) for fixing in the wheelhouse or taping to a bulkhead for easy reference.

Meaning of terms used in forecasting

The language of forecasters has reasonably precise meanings, and it will help you when making a weather chart to have an understanding of each phrase or term used.

Time has three categories:

Term	Meaning
Imminent	within six hours
Soon	six to twelve hours
Later	more than twelve hours

The behaviour of the barometer may be described in short phrases, particularly when the general synopsis is given or reports from coastal stations are put at the end of a forecast, and the general meanings are:

Phrase	Meaning
Area of low pressure	unstable and changing weather
Steady rise	good weather approaching

Phrase	*Meaning*
Rapid rise	good weather might not last
Area of high pressure	continuing stable weather
Steady fall	bad weather coming slowly
Falling rapidly	bad weather coming soon
Rising slowly	little change expected
Falling slowly	little change in near future
Steady	no change expected in near future

Other terms used in forecasts have the following meanings:

Term	*Meaning*
Anticyclone	a "high"; generally a sign of good weather
Backing	an anticlockwise wind change
Cyclonic	wind moving anticlockwise in the northern hemisphere around a low-pressure area
Front	a line of separation between warm and cold air masses
Isobars	lines drawn through positions having the same barometric pressure
Precipitation	usually rain, but can mean snow, sleet or hail
Ridge	an extension of a high-pressure area which sticks out in the manner of a mountain ridge
Secondary depression	isobars around a depression are often not symmetrical; bulges and distortions are called secondary depressions

Term	Meaning
Shower	rain of short duration, often with clear periods between each successive shower
Sleet	melting snow and rain falling together
Trough	the valley line in a low-pressure area, and the opposite of a ridge
Veering	a change of wind in a clockwise direction

Visibility is defined in the following terms:

Term	Meaning
Good	more than 5 miles
Moderate	2 to 5 miles
Poor	1100 yards to 2 miles
Fog	less than 1100 yards.

Conventional signs

The fastest, and correct, way to record wind speeds on a weather map is to have a dot as the location, a line from it showing wind direction (where the wind is coming *from*) and markings at the end of the line to show strength. In Fig. 18 it may be seen that a short bar means 5 knots of wind, and a long bar is 10 knots. Three long bars and a short one mean 35 knots, and a triangle looking a little like a flag marking the hole on a green means 50 knots of wind. Where greater precision is required you may draw a circle rather than make a dot and put the actual wind speed within it. As a rule, the wind speeds will be

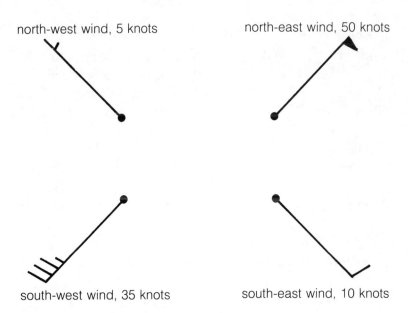

north-west wind, 5 knots

north-east wind, 50 knots

south-west wind, 35 knots

south-east wind, 10 knots

Fig. 18   Wind markings

associated with coastal weather stations whose positions are already shown on the outline map.

Making the weather map

Pads containing outline weather maps usually consist of two facing pages with the left-hand page for data and the right having the map itself. (The type used here is obtainable from the Royal Yachting Association.) As the forecast is read out you will be busy filling in the left-hand side, and grouping the data in the way shown in Fig. 19. The drawing of the map is best accomplished in two stages. Fig. 20 shows the map with the weather stations having the same barometer reading linked as a preliminary and the centre of the depression sketched in; Fig. 21 has the whole process complete.

R. MET. SOC./R.Y.A. METMAP

GENERAL SYNOPSIS	at ....!355.......... G̶M̶T̶/BST ....
LOW N SHANNON 985 MVG.SLY. NE LITTLE CHANGE	

Gales	SEA AREA FORECAST	Wind	Weather	Visibility
/	Viking			
/	N. Utsire			
/	S. Utsire			
/	Forties			
/	Cromarty	SE6 → G8 ?9 later	occ R/Sh	Mod / Gd
/	Forth			P→coast
	Tyne			
/	Dogger			
	Fisher			
	German Bight	SE5/6 inc 7 occ	occ R/Sh	"
	Humber			
	Thames			
	Dover	SE→SW 5/6 loc 7	R/Sh	Mod / Gd
	Wight			
	Portland			
	Plymouth	S/SW 4/5 occ 6	Sh	Gd
	Biscay			
	Trafalgar	SW4→5/6	Sh	Gd
	Finisterre			
	Sole			
	Lundy			
	Fastnet	S/SW 5 occ 6	Sh	Gd
	Irish Sea			
	Shannon	Var → mly var 5/7	Sh	Gd
/	Rockall			
/	Malin			
/	Hebrides	E/NE 6/8 occ 9	occ R/Sh	Mod / Gd
	Minches			
	Bailey			
	Fair Isle	E/SE 6/8 ?9 in Sth	occ Sh	Mod / Gd
	Faeroes			
	SE Iceland	E/NE 5/6 ?8 later	wintry Sh	Gd

COASTAL REPORTS (Shipping Bulletin) at 1100 BST G̶M̶T̶	Wind Direction	Force	Weather	Visibility	Pressure	Trend	COASTAL REPORTS (Inshore Waters) at .... BST GMT						
							Boulmer						
							Bridlington						
							Walton on the Naze						
Tiree	SE/E	6	Hze	5M	997	↓	St Catherine's Point						
Butt of Lewis	NE	7	R	1M	O2	↓	Mumbles						
Sumburgh	E'ly	6		8M	97	↓	Valley						
St Abb's Head	SE	6	Mist	1M	O5	↓	Blackpool						
Dowsing	SE	6	"	1M	O6	↓	Corsewall Point						
Dover	S	5		5M	O7	→	Larne						
Royal Sovereign	SE/S	5		"	O6	↓	Killough						
Channel L.V.	S/SW	5		11M	O2	→	Orlock Head						
Land's End	SE	4		22M	999	↓	Prestwick						
Valentia	S/SE	5	Hze	14M	992	→	Benbecula						
Ronaldsway	SE	4		13M	995	→	Stornoway						
Malin Head	SE	5		32M	995	→	Lerwick						
Jersey	S/SE	4		15M	O3	↓	Wick						
7.88							Aberdeen						
							Leuchars						

(Metmap reproduced by kind permission of the Royal Yachting Association)

Fig. 19 Recording forecast data

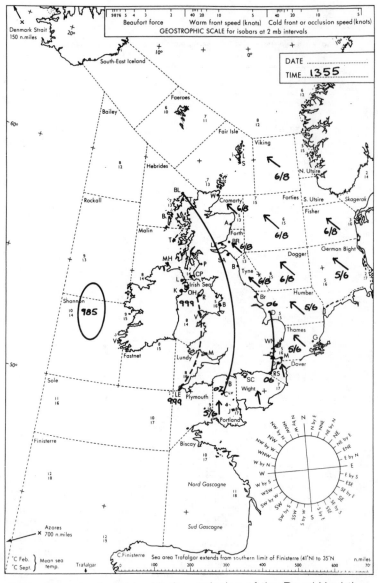

(Metmap reproduced by kind permission of the Royal Yachting Association)

Fig. 20   Putting in lines joining places of equal atmospheric pressure

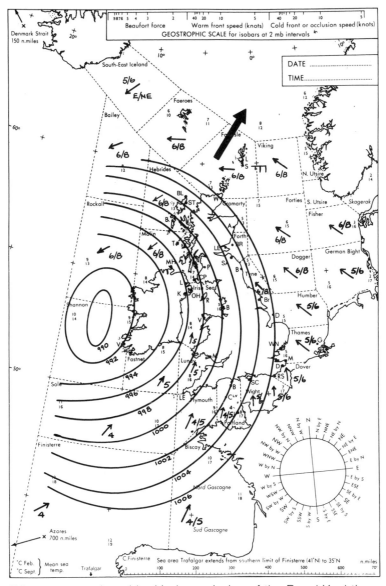

(Metmap reproduced by kind permission of the Royal Yachting Association)

Fig. 21   Rough sketch of the depression taken from the shipping forecast

What does Fig. 21 tell us? Well, that depends where you are at the time, and we will take three instances.

The first yacht is berthed in the Thames and is ready to start for Holland. South-south-east winds are being experienced at the moment, and the forecast has given the strengths as Five and Six, occasionally Seven. The depression is slow-moving, and it looks like a day in port for today. What about tomorrow? The north-east shift of the depression *might* bring the winds for Portland, Plymouth and Biscay nearer, and they have a southerly component. A start early tomorrow morning is a distinct possibility, and the skipper resolves to put his alarm clock on to get the 0555 forecast.

The next yacht is in the port of Whitby and comfortably aground on thick mud as the south-easter screams overhead, and her owner's plan is to work his way south. What can he expect tomorrow? Certainly a bit less wind: probably about Force Five, but it will have a lot of south in it and he may well decide to give it best for the time being.

The last yacht is moored at Lezardrieux and, as the holiday is coming to an end, the crew are looking for a homeward run. Being on the border of Plymouth and Portland for forecast purposes, they note that the forecast is Force Four and Five, occasionally Six, for both areas. The wind is fair, and the visibility good. It means an overnight passage, but does the weather map look encouraging? The low-pressure area is moving away; Biscay has the same winds – but without any mention of an occasional Six – and the pressure will rise. The skipper closes his log-book with a snap. "Cast off in about twenty minutes . . .?" he murmurs. "Time to head for home."

Chapter Four
THE COMING WIND

"And the coming wind did roar more loud,
And the sails did sigh like sedge;
And the rain poured down from one black cloud;
The Moon was on its edge."

From The Rime of the Ancient Mariner *by*
Samuel Taylor Coleridge, 1772–1834

In this chapter you will find a great deal about what combination of sails may be employed to meet specific weather conditions, and not much about engines. The reason is that in rough water sail is *more* reliable, as the Royal National Lifeboat Institution statistics show. In 1987, one-third of all launches were to assist yachts in distress on account of machinery failure or fouled propellors: only 4 per cent of launches were in respect of yachts with sail or mast failure. Sail is much more likely to get you out of trouble, and what follows is geared in that direction with engines having their proper auxiliary role. The five types of craft to be dealt with are the sloop and cutter with one mast and the yawl, ketch and schooner with two. The illustrations in this chapter show old-fashioned reefing points on sails, but these are chiefly symbolic as many boats have roller- or slab-reefing systems to achieve the equivalents of a single or double deep-reef, while roller headsails and mainsails enable a reduction of sail without the necessity of working forward in rough weather.

The sloop

In Fig. 22 the amount and type of sail that should be carried by a sloop in winds between Force Three and Force Eight is set out, but it needs emphasising that these combinations are for a strong boat with a large crew and a long way to go. Lighter-manned craft in no particular hurry may opt for comfort rather than speed, so that in Force Five they carry the sails for Force Six, and so on. Not much comment is required for the top two examples in Fig. 22, except to say that at the upper end of the range for Force Four – say 15 knots of wind – a close-hauled sloop may find its rail in the water and the crew thinking of a headsail change. In Force Five conditions there are two possibilities: either keep the full main and change down to a small genoa – as shown – or follow racing practice by keeping the large genoa up and reducing the size of the mainsail. In Force Six there is the choice of putting in a single reef in the mainsail and hoisting the Number One jib or, if racing, try the Number Three genoa with a double reef in the main. At Force Seven it *has* to be a double reef in the main and a smaller jib, but in the early stages of Force Eight it is possible to try six rolls or a very deep reef in the main and a Number Two jib before shifting to the rig given in Fig. 22 – a trysail and storm jib or spitfire.

The two things to take into account when making sail changes are keeping helm balance and avoiding excessive reductions which bring the boat speed down to a wallowing gait that bears its own brand of danger by slowing the craft too much. Every boat is different, but the ideal is to retain a small amount of weather helm with each successive reduction. If lee helm is detected following a reduction you must either set more sail aft or cut down the size

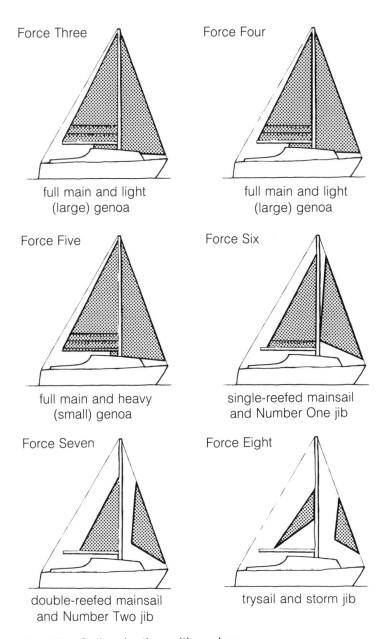

Force Three
full main and light
(large) genoa

Force Four
full main and light
(large) genoa

Force Five
full main and heavy
(small) genoa

Force Six
single-reefed mainsail
and Number One jib

Force Seven
double-reefed mainsail
and Number Two jib

Force Eight
trysail and storm jib

Fig. 22   Sail reduction with a sloop

of the fore triangle. The heading can also be important. Going down-wind it is helpful to have more sail set forward so as to correct any tendency to broach, while a yacht on a close reach will need plenty of push from the main-sail to stop the bows being knocked aside by the waves. High-cut sails are less likely to be filled with solid water, and some of the smaller headsails should be fitted with a wire pendant to achieve greater above-deck height.

The cutter

There are two main versions of the cutter: the older, traditional type has a long bowsprit carrying a jib set outside the forestaysail and, sometimes, a topsail set above the mainsail which is itself suspended from a gaff. In this rig the mainsail is often held to the mast by hoops and laced onto boom and gaff while the outer headsail is carried out on a traveller to the end of the bowsprit. Having owned a gaff cutter for ten years, I can say, with feeling, that a skipper's first concern when the wind pipes up is to get the topsail down before anything jams and the jib in while it is still manageable. Then, and only then, is the cutter reduced to the rig of a gaff sloop, and sail reduction may follow the pattern for a sloop which has just been described. However, most modern cutters are Bermudan-rigged and similar in appearance to a sloop except that they have an extra stay inside the forestay and can set two headsails at the same time. Some craft have a removeable inner stay and are known, somewhat unkindly, as slutters, but perhaps the expression cutter-rigged sloop is to be preferred.

The chief advantage that the cutter has over the sloop is that as there are usually two sails set when a reduction becomes necessary you have one still pulling as the change takes place so that there need be very little loss of speed.

Further, alteration entails no change of course and there is a better wardrobe of sails than with a sloop. In Fig. 23 you can see the alternative headsails that may be used once the genoa has been taken in. The staysail *and* the yankee may be kept up with a fair wind, but generally the high-cut yankee alone is in place for winds of Force Five and Force Six with a mainsail reduction for the higher wind strength. Note in Fig. 23 that with Force

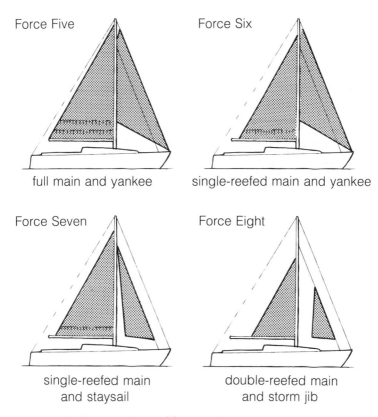

Force Five — full main and yankee

Force Six — single-reefed main and yankee

Force Seven — single-reefed main and staysail

Force Eight — double-reefed main and storm jib

Fig. 23   Sail reduction with a cutter

Seven and Force Eight winds the reductions have the effect of keeping the sails close together and either side of the mast or, as the naval architects have it, around the Total Centre of Effort (TCE). Quite a different approach is taken with some of the two-masted craft, but in the case of the yawl the TCE is still focused on the foremast.

The yawl

This is a two-masted vessel with a tall mainmast and a relatively short mizzen-mast. Technically, the yawl differs from the ketch in having the smaller mast astern of the rudder post and steering gear while the ketch has its second mast forward of the rudder post; the real difference, however, is that the yawl uses its mizzen sail for steering, not for driving. Thus, as in Fig. 24, the yawl discards its aft sail fairly quickly and thereafter behaves like a sloop. As a rule, the mizzen-sail in a yawl does not have provision for reefing as, unlike a ketch, the mast is not strongly stayed and, in the manner of Thames sailing barges which also have small mizzens, once stowed it is stowed for good. I have shown a trysail with a storm jib for Force Eight conditions, but most yawl owners seem to prefer rolling down the mainsail to the sail number rather than carrying and fitting a trysail. I will say more about this sail later on, but it seems that many yawl owners subscribe to John Mellor's strongly-held opinion that trysails are "cumbersome, awkward and difficult to rig, useless for sailing to windward", and that "the best place for a trysail is in the garden shed". The yawl rig combines the best features of the cutter and ketch so that, in light weather, the yawl lies closer to the wind and will beat to windward in a most satisfactory way. Downwind, the ketch has the edge.

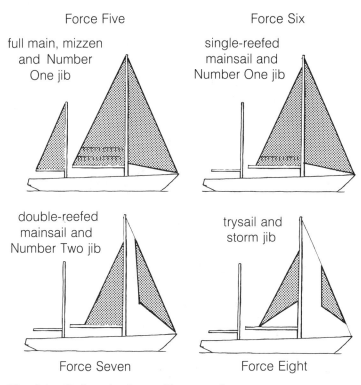

Force Five

full main, mizzen
and Number
One jib

Force Six

single-reefed
mainsail and
Number One jib

double-reefed
mainsail and
Number Two jib

trysail and
storm jib

Force Seven

Force Eight

Fig. 24 Sail reduction with a yawl

The ketch

This rig evolved originally in fishing craft, and was believed to save the expense of one crewman. It has the priceless advantage that when the wind comes up a light crew of, say, two people can simply drop the mainsail and jill along under headsail and mizzen while further plans are made. In my old ketch with just two of us on board and no great way to go it often pays to leave the mainsail stowed and finish the trip under jib, mizzen and engine. With a stronger crew and some distance to voyage the sail changes follow the order in Fig. 25. In the

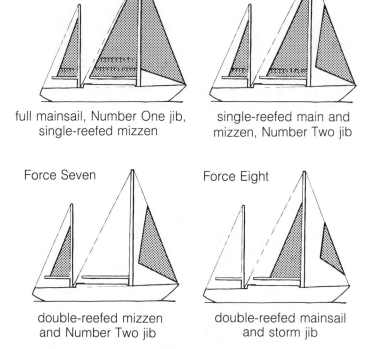

Force Five

full mainsail, Number One jib,
single-reefed mizzen

Force Six

single-reefed main and
mizzen, Number Two jib

Force Seven

double-reefed mizzen
and Number Two jib

Force Eight

double-reefed mainsail
and storm jib

Fig. 25   Sail reduction with a ketch

first step from Force Four to Force Five the genoa is
replaced by a large jib and a single reef is put in the
mizzen, and in the next change the main is reduced and
the Number Two jib goes up. At Force Seven the jib can
stay and the main comes down altogether. I have shown
in Fig. 25 that the mizzen is further reduced, but in some
cases it can stay single-reefed for the time being. When a
fresh gale is blowing it is necessary to make the most
radical adjustment by re-hoisting the deep-reefed main,
discarding the mizzen altogether and shifting to a storm
jib.

Gaff ketches follow a similar range of reduction, with the difference that topsails will have disappeared early in the story and outer jibs and staysails may also have been dowsed once Force Five is reached. With a gaff ketch it is often advantageous to hold on to a deep-reefed mizzen all the way because having some sail set aft counteracts wind pressure on the bowsprit and rigging. In both types, division of sail into penny packets and the possession of two masts makes for easy sail-handling and setting-up a jury rig if something goes wrong. Best of all, many ketches with well-balanced canvas will sail themselves for much of the time.

The schooner

The schooner is an American invention, and when the first one was built and launched in 1713 a bystander exclaimed: "Oh, look how she *scoons!*" as she slid into the water. The designer responded, "A *scooner* let her be", thus naming the rig for posterity.

There are gaff-rigged schooners with all the chief sails, including the headsail, on booms, and topsail schooners with one or more square sails set on yards on the foremast, but the commonest yacht type is the staysail schooner shown in Fig. 26. In light airs, a big genoa is put up forward and a curious sail, called a fisherman, set above the staysail that occupies the space between the two masts; once the wind gets up, however, the two big pullers are the staysail and the headsail which is, confusingly, often called the forestaysail. Note that in Fig. 26 the amidships, or mizzen, staysail is the one that does not budge, with successive reductions made in the size of the mainsail between Forces Five and Six, and at each change of wind force in the case of the headsail. Schooners are at

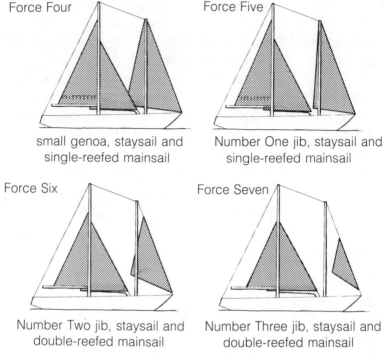

Force Four
small genoa, staysail and
single-reefed mainsail

Force Five
Number One jib, staysail and
single-reefed mainsail

Force Six
Number Two jib, staysail and
double-reefed mainsail

Force Seven
Number Three jib, staysail and
double-reefed mainsail

Fig. 26   Sail reduction with a schooner

their best with beam winds, and do not point well, but
once they have a heading of about 60° to the true wind
they can be very fast indeed. The rig remains extremely
popular in the West Indies where progression up and
down the strings of islands is facilitated by a beam wind
for most of the year.

Reefing techniques

Shortening sail in a hurry has already been mentioned
when discussing the ketch rig, and sometimes the most
effective thing to do when there is a sudden freshening of

the wind is to drop a sail. A squall will often compel this type of instant reefing, but which sail to drop? The temptation, especially when running, is to drop the main and keep the headsail, but this is not always such a good idea as it seems because the TCE is upset and the mast comes under strain with all the push and pull of the wind at the top and no support from the mainsail. Drop the headsail by all means as an emergency tactic, and then think about a change, reefing the main or re-hoisting the original sail. The mechanics of reefing depend to some extent on the gear fitted to the boat, and each system has its own peculiar problems.

Slab-reefing

This is one of the cheapest ways of creating a reefing system, because, once the sail has got cringles, eyelets or reef points that are usually sewn in by the maker, the rest of the gear is on the boom in the shape of blocks, fixed, clam or jam cleats, or reefing horns. To reef, it is first necessary to slacken the kicking strap and tension the topping lift so that when the halliard is eased away the boom does not come crashing down on the crew. The halliard is eased away, and the leech and luff pendants are kept taut while the surplus sail gathers under the boom. Fig. 27 has the lowering process completed, and the next step is to hook on, or tie up the luff pendant, and then harden in the leech pendant and make it fast.

If the reef is a temporary one, it is quite permissible to let the surplus sail flutter beneath the boom until the next change takes place, but where the sail is fitted with reef points they may be tied around the sausage of surplus sail gathered on the boom. It is *not* a good idea to tie reef points around the boom itself for this tends to distort the

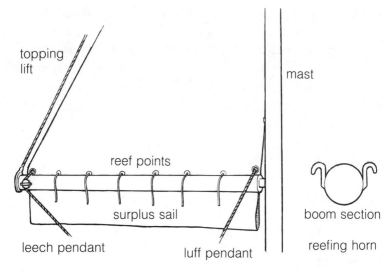

topping lift

mast

reef points

surplus sail

boom section

leech pendant

luff pendant

reefing horn

Fig. 27   Pulling down a reef

sail, and if there are no points but a line of eyelets across the sail a lacing line may be put through them and wound round-and-round the boom. The reefing horn (shown on the right in Fig. 27) makes life easy for the crew as they merely have to hook on the luff cringle when it is down far enough and then concentrate on getting the leech tight and secured.

The finer points of reefing may be briefly described. You must not forget to take the pins out of the mast that release the luff of the sail from the track before lowering, or neglect to ease the topping lift and adjust the kicking strap and downhaul afterwards. Jam cleats on the boom to take the pendants save time, and a small double-whip tackle on the leech pendant will get it really tight. The reef knot does not always hold as well as it should under tension, and the cure is to use the reverse surgeon's knot shown in Fig. 28, which is essentially a reef knot with an

Fig. 28   The reverse surgeon's knot

extra turn taken in the first (lower) twist of the joined points.

Roller-reefing

This method has two great advantages, and one draw-back. The prime attraction of roller-reefing is that, in theory, you can have an infinitely variable amount of sail presented to the wind, from one-sixth in the worst of weather to nine-tenths when one or two rolls will do. Second, no reef points are needed. The drawback is that it often requires three crewmen to get a clean reef in the sail; one lowering away on the halliard, one working the handle and a third hauling back all the time on the leech to ensure that wrinkles do not form as the rolls go in. Additionally, with a deep reef in the sail there is the vexed problem of boom droop caused by the uneven distribution of the rolled canvas and the roped luff on the boom. Older types of booms had a wooden wedge near the outboard end to counteract droop; with modern metal tubes of equal circumference the best solution is to have a taped rather than a roped luff to the mainsail to cut down bulkiness at the inboard end of the boom.

If you want to put in a reef before leaving the mooring

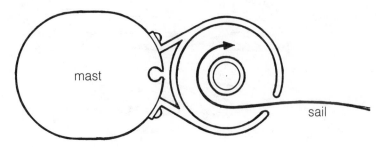

Fig. 29   On-mast reefing

it is best to haul the sail right up, and then wind down. As in the case of slab-reefing, the pins must come out to release the slides from the track, but the boom-attached kicking strap has to come off altogether. When shaking out a reef you will have to use the handle again, feed the slides back into the track and clip on the kicking strap once more. There is a second type of roller-reefing that works in the vertical rather than the horizontal plane with the sail wound into the mast rather than round the boom, and many of the inexpensive systems are bolt-ons that take the form of an additional tube attached to the mast. A sectional view of one type appears in Fig. 29, and you may see variants with no outer casing and the rolled sail in plain view behind the mainmast. In either case, furling is accomplished by pulling on a cord which engages in an endless groove and rolls the sail around a rotating rod.

Headsail-reefing

Roller headsails are almost too well known to require description, but the principle is that of the spring-loaded roller blind with reduction and sail-setting accomplished by pulling on one of two ropes or cords. A slotted foil holds the luff, and having this sail rolled up on the forestay or foil most of the time saves valuable below-deck space. However, there are no pleasures without pains, and roller headsails have three demerits. The wind will sometimes get its fingers into a rolled sail when the boat is in harbour and do damage; they do not set well in high winds when the semi-rigid luff starts to bend, and they jam. In very light weather a jammed roller headsail can be lashed around its stay or housing in the same way as a mainsail is tied to a boom, but in rough conditions it will be necessary to take off one headsail sheet, coil the other, and motor round in circles passing the coiled sheet until the flogging sail is lashed tightly. Horrific tales, some probably apocryphal, are told of yachts in this predicament that had to run down-wind for long distances before being able to muzzle recalcitrant headsails, and in this predicament it might be best to let them flap and adopt Solent Rig to get out of trouble. This is a well-reefed main-sail and engine running at maximum revolutions, and gets its name from being seen so frequently off the Needles on Sunday afternoons. When the prevailing south-westerly is blowing, many owners out for the day will fight their way down to the Needles under Solent Rig and then turn round with free sheets to get back in time for tea.

This chapter has been all about what to do, but now I want to get down to something much more important – exactly how to do it.

Chapter Five
STOW THAT JIB!

" 'We'll have to get the small jib set and put a couple of reefs in the mainsail,' I shouted into the mate's ear. 'Help me stow that jib!' "

From The Magic of the Swatchways *(1932) by Maurice Griffiths*

The three maxims to bear in mind when shortening sail are to do it early, do it safely and do it systematically. With a worsening weather forecast the prudent skipper will so arrange his sails that they are ready in the right order on a spare bunk and, if in harbour, start with a cautious reef in the main. It is always so much easier to shake out a reef at sea than to put one in. Foredeck work requires pre-programming, and some essential parts of the programme follow.

The jib sheet fastenings should be "soft" rather than "hard" – knots and toggles rather than shackles or clips, and in the top part of Fig. 30 there are two suggestions for achieving a "soft" connection whereby sail-changers are not brained by swinging lumps of metal. The bagging of sails needs to be thought out in a sensible way, and I would suggest that "three corners out" is the best method with the head, tack and clew sticking out a few inches beyond the mouth of the bag and the rest of the sail lashed within it. The folding of sails is only justifiable when they go home for winter storage; with the "three corners out" technique it is easy to secure one or more hanks to the forestay while dealing with the sail that is

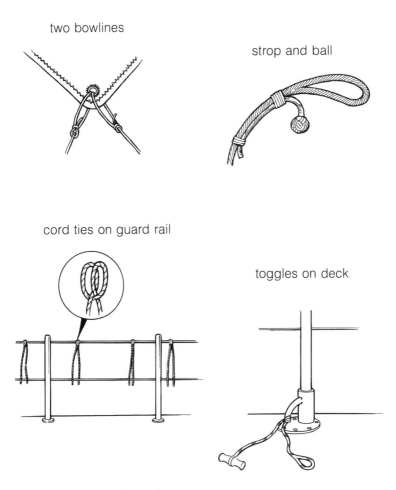

two bowlines

strop and ball

cord ties on guard rail

toggles on deck

Fig. 30   Foredeck work

being replaced, and make fast the head with the sail still in the bag and not billowing about the deck. Some sails not in current use, but likely to be required during the voyage, may have to be secured on the foredeck in such a way that wind or sea will not carry them off, and two suggestions appear in the lower part of Fig. 30. Clovehitched lengths of cord on the top guardrail act as ready-use sail ties, while toggles at the foot of the stanchions will hold a sail, yet cut down windage. On the subject of cloth sail ties, it must be kept in mind that short ones are not a lot of good because you want to get at least two turns around a boom and sail, or a foredeck sausage, and that means they should be some 2 metres long. White terylene ties, about 1 inch wide, will not mark or wrinkle sails, and they should be taken home for a scrub and iron each winter.

A jib downhaul is a useful adjunct when sail-changing, and there are various types. The simplest is a cord rove through the piston hanks and tied to the head of the sail to act in equal and opposite fashion to the halliard, and another idea is to have a similar light line with its lower half looped across the sail, as in Fig. 31. This latter device has the advantage that you can exert downward pressure without having to go right up into the eyes of the ship to yank on the cord. The length of halliards is important, because nothing makes the crewman's job easier than being able to unclip from the old headsail and, with a reasonably immobile halliard at full stretch, clip on to a new one or to the pulpit without having to return to the mast for adjustment. At the mast end of a halliard a pre-prepared handy knot or loop enables a solo crewman to make roughly fast to a cleat before moving forward to haul down. It is also particularly irritating to make one's way up forward from the cockpit and then have to return for a winch or reefing handle, so that a pouch attached to the mast – see Fig. 31 – with the handles secured by shock cord is what estate agents would call a desirable additional feature. The bringing of sail-bags up to the foredeck is a task for active, practising cowards, for the best technique is to shackle on to the

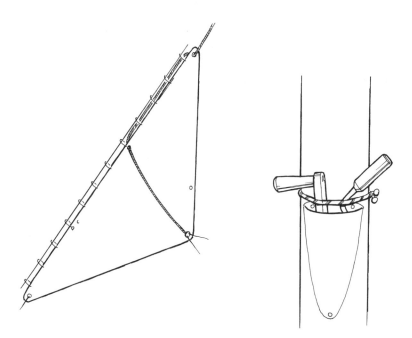

Fig. 31   Downhaul and mast pouch

safety wire or lifeline, adopt a humble crouch and *drag*
the bag behind you. Standing up is foolish, and the same
may be said of all foredeck activity where sitting and
kneeling are perfectly acceptable behaviour and not at all
unmanly. The bagging of old sails is best accomplished
below decks, and it is a good idea to plan to bundle the
old sail, and the new sail-bag, down the forehatch for
later attention.

The headsail change

A stable working platform is the first requirement, and
the simplest way of providing the right conditions for a
headsail change is to run down-wind with the boom well

out so that the mainsail blankets the headsail and the deck is steady and level. Rigging a preventer will prevent an involuntary gybe, and this is provided by rigging up a long rope – quite often the longest warp – to run from the boom to a foredeck block and back to the cockpit in the manner set out in Fig. 32. With the main sheet pulling one way and the preventer the other the boom will not shift, even if the boat sails by the lee with the wind on the wrong quarter. When all the weight is out of the headsail and the yacht is running smoothly with a dry deck the

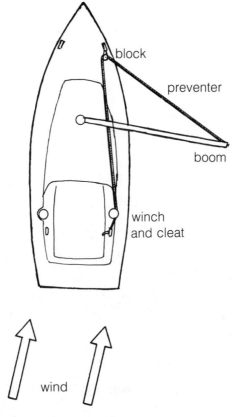

Fig. 32 Setting up a preventer

crew can go forward, clipped on, as the foresheets are sheeted in hard. The act of lowering a sail cannot really be separated from hoisting its replacement, for the first step is to take the tension off the halliard and remove one or two hanks near the deck. Hank on enough of the new sail to make sure it won't blow away, *but do not take it out of its bag at this stage.* Haul down the old jib or genoa, slackening the sheets as it comes down, release all the hanks and the sheets and transfer the snap shackle at the head of the sail to either the new head or, temporarily, to the pulpit. At this stage, the old sail is merely held by the tack; the new sail by a few hanks and the snap shackle at its head. Unshackle the tack, and get rid of the old sail.

The new sail can now be prepared for hoisting, but first, like Mrs Beeton, you have to find your tack, which is generally at the corner with the makers' name nearby. Shackle or clip it on, not forgetting that if this sail is smaller than its predecessor it might need a pendant to give it extra height. Put the piston hanks on the forestay in order from the tack to the head, making sure that they all go on the same way to avoid a twist in the luff when the sail is raised. Discard the sail-bag when enough hanks are made fast, but get it down the forehatch or lash it to the rail to stop it blowing away. Before you put the sheets on, run your hand along the foot of the sail to make sure it is not twisted, and take a last look at the head of the sail and the halliard to see that it will run freely and has not fouled the forestay or the shrouds. The clip connecting the head of the sail and the halliard can now be fitted, if it had been made fast hitherto on the pulpit, or re-fitted if it had just been attached to the head earlier for holding purposes. The boat is still running down-wind, and the headsail hoister is ready to start work.

As a rule, you will not need the winch handle at the

beginning, and hand-over-hand will get the new sail most of the way up. Wind the wire or rope of the halliard round the drum of the winch two or three times, and then "tail" the free end away horizontally. It helps to have a second crewman tailing away on this free end while you insert the handle and haul the sail tight on its stay. The only things likely to go wrong at this stage are losing tension on the drum while fastening the halliard to the cleat, or getting the handle stuck. In the latter case, there is a pear-shaped knob at the business end of the handle which can be jiggled to free the star-sectioned barrel at the same end of the handle from its socket in the winch. At the cockpit end, the sheet will be brought in taut when the crewmen clear the foredeck, and this is just the time to get a riding turn on the winch. The sail will be flogging about, and it is most unwise to try to remove the whole set of turns to start again. Find an odd piece of rope and clove-hitch it to the part of the sheet under tension. Take the strain on this auxiliary sheet and make it fast to something substantial – as in the right-hand part of Fig. 33. When the turns are out the odd piece of rope can be undone again as the winch resumes the pull of the sheet. Whatever you do, keep your fingers off the barrel until the weight is off it, and on no account use them to pry under the jammed sheet and pluck out a free end: it won't work and is dangerous. Note that in Fig. 33 the ends of the sheets have figure-of-eight knots in them. These make sure that if, by chance, you let go of the cockpit end of the sheets they will only travel as far as the block on the sheet tracks and may be readily recovered. This type of down-wind hoist does not go well without mast winches, and the alternative is to come briefly head to wind under the engine to take the pressure of the hanks off the forestay while the last of the sail goes up.

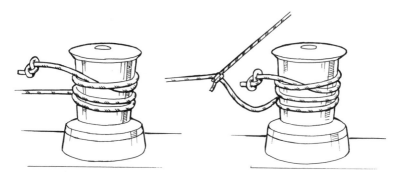

Fig. 33   Taking out a riding turn

Heaving-to for mainsail reefing

It seems logical that as the mainsail protected the fore-deck area during headsail changes that the headsail should protect the main in its turn. The dual motive in heaving-to when reefing the mainsail is get some shelter for people working on the main from the backed headsail and to slow the boat right down. The basics of heaving-to appear in Fig. 34: in (a) the boat has just begun to turn into the wind as if it was going about on the other tack; at (b) the boat has gone round through the eye of the wind, but the headsail sheet has been left severely alone so that the sail is now filled with wind and tightly suspended between forestay and starboard shroud. It is usual to slacken the main sheet somewhat at this stage, and the tiller is tied down to leeward so that any forward progress from the sails is converted into an up-wind impulse. Fig. 34(c) shows what happens in the long term when hove-to. The yacht drifts down-wind and makes a "smooth" to windward, and it see-saws back and forward as the wind first works on both sails to give forward drive and then encounters the backed headsail to thrust the boat back again. For a craft with a deep forefoot and a

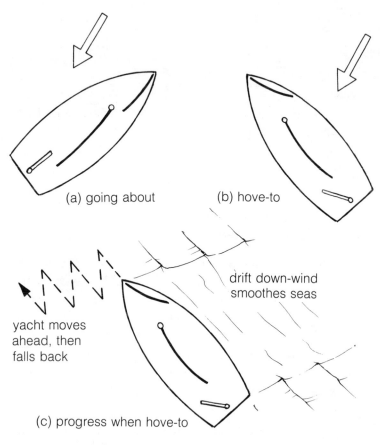

(a) going about   (b) hove-to

yacht moves
ahead, then
falls back

drift down-wind
smoothes seas

(c) progress when hove-to

Fig. 34   Heaving-to

long keel heaving-to is a manoeuvre well worth practising.
It steadies the boat miraculously, has a dramatic impact
on living conditions, enables a tired crew to have a meal
or just sort themselves out and, as in this case, greatly
facilitates a sail change.

The procedure for mainsail reefing has been described
in the last chapter, and the only supplementary advice I
want to give is in relation to making the reduced sail set
well. First, it will pull badly if it is slack in the luff, so

that after the halliard has been sweated up as hard as it will go you *must* get that last bit under control by a savage heave on the downhaul. Some lower battens may have to come out, and they will need numbering to make sure they go back in the right order. If they stay in, be certain that they roll in parallel to the boom with roller-reefing. The topping lift may have been taut while reefing went on; now is the time to give it some slack. The kicking strap will certainly be loose, or even removed altogether, at this stage, and as this piece of equipment controls mainsail twist and prevents the (lifting) Chinese gybe it is a good move to tighten it up. Wrinkles radiating from the reef points are signs of uneven tension, and if there is billowing in between it means that you did not stretch the leech enough as the reef went in. Once you have the sail

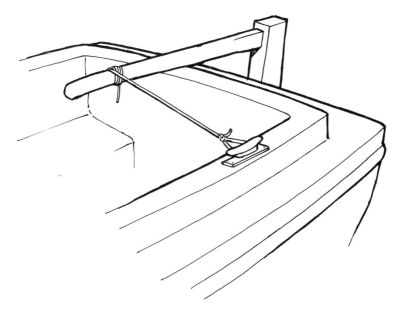

Fig. 35   Tiller relieving line

looking right you may unlash the tiller or wheel, let the jib fly and sail on. The tiller relieving line used when hove-to will also hold the yacht on course for quite long periods if you need to leave the helm and, as you may see from Fig. 35, it is a device at the lower end of the technology spectrum.

Fore-reaching

We have seen earlier that heaving-to was a good manoeuvre for long-keeled yachts but, of course, a great number of modern craft have a different underwater profile and do not heave-to at all well. The alternative is fore-reaching – a kind of not-quite-hove-to technique where the headsail is pinned amidships using *both* sheets and the main left reasonably slack. The rudder position is of no great consequence, and indeed the helm can be left unattended for long periods. The yacht will jog along slowly at about 80° to the true wind, and there is leisure to change the area of the main with all hands employed. Fore-reaching is also useful when you have arrived on a strange coast before dawn and do not want to close the shore until you can see exactly where you are, or are awaiting a tide across a bar.

Steering shy

Many contemporary yachts are so designed that sail changes are best done with the wind forward of the beam, and when the going is heavy, the spray flying and the foredeck pitching, there may be an understandable reluctance on the part of the crew to get on with it. Steering shy means sheeting the sails as if for a close reach and then steering above the course for close hauled so that speed drops to a couple of knots and there is a lot of fluttering in the leeches, but not much progress. It has the advantage over fore-reaching and heaving-to in that no ground is lost to leeward – a powerful consideration in sea areas like the Thames Estuary where sandbanks grow under the lee gunwhale all the time. Steering shy can be employed for both headsail and mainsail reductions, although careful steering will be needed in the former case, and there is no disgrace in running the engine to keep the yacht on the right heading.

The trysail

In Fig. 22 and Fig. 24 I have shown a trysail as the proper sail to set on the mast of a sloop or yawl in Force Eight conditions, and it is time to amplify on its use. Except in an emergency situation (to be covered later) a trysail cannot be set "flying" – that is, supported at just the three corners – nor should it be attached to the boom but to the hull itself. In heavy seas a swinging boom is potentially lethal, and there are manifest advantages in putting the boom to sleep on a gallows, in a crutch or lashed down out of harm's way. The attachment of a trysail to the mast demands a separate track, and prefer-ably a separate halliard, because there is no way a crewman on tiptoe, with his arms above his head, is going to be able to stuff slides into a mainsail track whose first foot or two is obstructed by stowed sail and mainsail slides. There is no "gate" for him to start from, and if he takes off the mainsail slides the wind will billow the sail and buffet him about. The track for the trysail should be offset to the main track; begin below the crosstrees and end at about where the headboard of the mainsail lies when it is furled. The clew should be secured to two three-part tackles stretching right aft, with a tail running forward to the cockpit winches – as in Fig. 36. A down-haul completes the gear.

With a well-set trysail and storm jib a yacht should lie at about 75° to the true wind and will forereach at about 1½ knots.

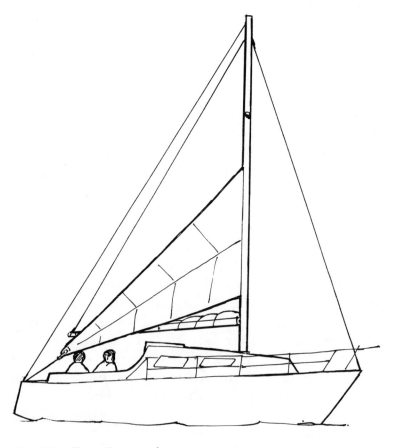

Fig. 36   Trysail at work

Emergency trysail

Ocean wanderers are the only people certain to have trysails in their sail wardrobe, and the coasting yachtsman is often going to have to improvise. After exhausting the possibilities offered by reducing the main it will have to come down and be replaced by a reversed jib – as shown in Fig. 37. The emergency trysail has no slides on its new luff, and the halliard and downhaul will have to be passed around the mast to hold the sail in place as it is hoisted. The clew – formerly the tack – has to be secured to the end of the boom to exert enough force to get the sail taut, and control will be exercised by the mainsheets. Alterna-

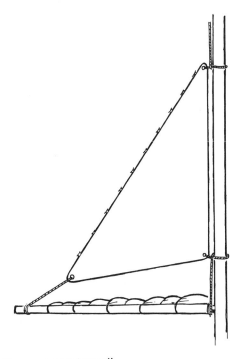

Fig. 37   Emergency trysail

tively, I once tried a storm jib hanked onto a tightly-stretched wire halliard the normal way up, but had to sheet it right aft in the same way as the orthodox trysail to get the correct lead. Did it work well? Only moderately well, I fear, because of the difficulties experienced in getting the foot of the sail tight enough.

The storm jib

This sail gets so little use normally that it tends to be in tip-top condition with its stitches standing proud and its cringles still shiny. The first essential is to get it up high; a wire pendant of some 3 feet or more will be adequate for the purpose. Craft that normally rely on a roller headsail will need an extra stay *outside* the roller to carry a storm jib, and cutters have the advantage in that they can set one on the inner stay. This is the last sail a boat will carry after going through the whole gamut of changing and reefing for, as we shall see in the next chapter, what follows when the storm jib comes in is either "dodging" with the engine, running with no sail at all or "lying a-hull" – the last expedient of a hard-driven ship.

Chapter Six
"SEA ROOME ENOUGH"

"Making out from this danger, wee sounded one while seven fadome, then five fadome, then four fadome and lesse, againe deeper, immediately four fadome, then but three fadome, the sea going mightily and high. At last we recovered (God be thanked) in some despaire, to sea roome enough."

From The Voyage of Sir Humphrey Gilbert
(1583) by Edward Haie, gentleman

A yacht at sea that receives advice of rough weather has four choices. It can, as in the example used in Chapter Three, wait it out at anchor, confident that an improvement and a change of wind is on the way. It may make for the shelter of a port, sure in the knowledge that the entrance is easy, visibility will be good, there is plenty of water and the marks are unambiguous, there is time to get in before the weather deteriorates, and a safe berth may be found. The other alternatives are to stick to the original passage plan, or remain at sea with a modified plan. In these latter cases the essential factor is going to be "sea roome enough", for if the coming wind is going to pin the yacht against a lee shore the chances are that extreme measures might have to be tried.

In years gone by the ultimate tactic was deliberate beaching, as described in *The New Seaman's Guide and Coaster's Companion* of 1803. Speaking of the dangers of Lyme Bay, the authors commented bleakly that "fuch veffels as were embayed here, with the wind and fea high, and efpecially at the beginning of the ebb tide, to run aground upon the Chefil-bank; but, as that bank is very hard, being compofed of ftones, loofe fhingle, &c. this expedient is attended with imminent danger, and has, in many cafes, been fatal."

This kind of drama is avoided by excluding from the passage plan, or modified passage plan, any course that entails closing a low shore with a strong beam wind in poor visibility or being pinned between two headlands with rolling seas forcing the yacht towards the shore. The open sea is *always* safer than shallow water, but as the instinctive reaction to news of bad weather is to make for harbour it is best to start with an up-wind approach to a safe haven.

Tactical beating

The windward ability of yachts varies with their length, underwater shape, rig and sail plan, and is further curtailed by the strength of the wind and power of the waves. Very roughly, we can say that at Force Five a yacht will still make between 45° and 50° to the true wind; at Force Six perhaps 55° and at Force Seven about 60°. Racing yachts will do better than this; shoal draft craft may sag away to leeward and be hard put to it to make 80°. However, all types will benefit from an understanding of the "making" tack and lee-bowing a tide to get to an up-wind destination.

"Making" and losing tacks

A direct line is the shortest distance between two points, but when it is not possible to go that way it makes sense to go as near as may be – a principle outlined in Fig. 38. This is a fine-weather situation, and it is obvious that the

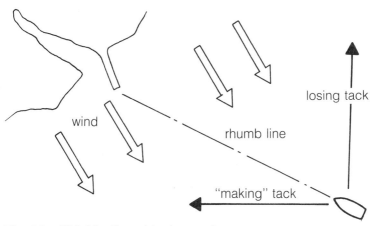

Fig. 38 "Making" and losing tacks

"making" tack at the bottom of the illustration will get the yacht into port sooner than the losing tack because the "making" tack is closest to the rhumb line. The angles will be broader in rough weather, and account must be taken of wind shifts. In Fig. 38 the wind is about north-north-westerly, and if it veers to north the yacht on the "making" tack can steer the rhumb line and go straight for home. On the other hand, if the wind backs south-westerly the yacht must go about at once for what was the losing tack now becomes the "making" tack. With the wind dead ahead there is neither a "making" or a losing tack; in Fig. 39 we have the "cone" approach with the yacht crossing the rhumb line in tacks of decreasing distance.

From a practical point of view, the "cone" approach to a port is best done using time rather than distance, so that the boat is put about by reference to the saloon clock. Crews get fed up staring at a shoreline that gets closer with infinite slowness, and it is a good move to tot up the time to be taken by all the tacks to come, add a bit

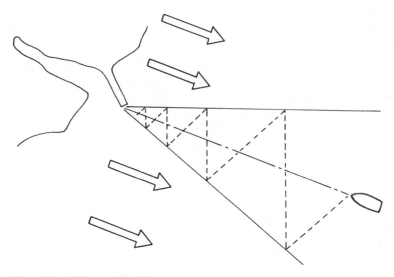

Fig. 39 "Cone" tacking

for leeway, and tell them what the ETA (estimated time of arrival) may be. If you get it exactly right your standing will increase 100 per cent. Fig. 39 is a rough-weather situation, with the yacht making no better than 60° to the wind, and the distance covered is about twice the direct route. In this particular plot the navigator has put the "cone" lines at 15° to the rhumb line, but if there is a long way to go the angle could well be wider to allow for longer tacks and greater intervals between bouts of sail-handling.

Lee-bowing the tide

When working to windward in a rising wind the tempta-tion is always to take the tack that runs with the tide, but this may not always be the quickest way there. In Fig. 40 two yachts start from a point in the Bay of the Seine heading for the Nab. The black yacht, on the right, goes

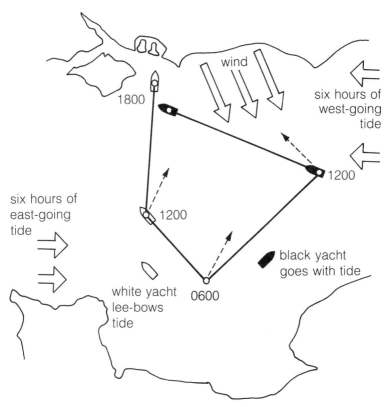

Fig. 40   Lee-bowing the tide

away on the port tack to take advantage of an east-going
tide and at noon goes about to carry the west-going tide.
The white yacht starts on a north-westerly heading, split-
ting the angle between tide and wind and taking the
thrust of the tide on her lee or port side. At noon it
appears that she is behind, but she again splits the wind
and tide angle to head a little east of north. On both legs
she is using the tide to counteract the push of the wind,
and the left-hand solid lines show her progress. The
result is that she reaches the Nab an hour before her
rival.

Steering to windward

A careless helmsman may lose 10 feet or so to leeward on every wave when steering in a rough sea, and when that figure is multiplied up over some hours it amounts to a couple of miles down-wind of a destination. There is a technique for keeping the boat moving *and* on approximate course which can be summed-up (with apologies to a well-known gospel tune) as "one wave at a time, sweet Jesus", because it means taking your eye off the compass and "reading" the waves. It is important not to let the big ones stop the boat dead in the water, so you bear away for these whoppers, while luffing up in the relatively quiet patches. Very occasionally, this rule is broken when an absolute monster curls up. To cut down the possibility of damage or injury this type may be met almost head-on and the risk of loss of headway is accepted. A warning shout to those below will be appreciated, and the same precaution should be taken when the wake of a large vessel is about to reach the hull. When your watch is over and you get below it is sensible to tell the navigator what you have been steering in the troughs and on the crests so that he can average out the course made good and still make an allowance for leeway.

Sail and motor

We are all motor-sailors nowadays, and there are occasions when prudence dictates that the engine should, at the very least, be switched on and ticking over. It is, in effect, the boat's electricity generating station so that in long periods of darkness, rain or during thunderstorms when there is heavy demand for lighting it will replace lost amps. Similarly, a self-steerer, radar, depth-sounder and VHF may be in constant use, with a corresponding decline in battery capacity. Batteries charge faster under load, and a boat nearing safety could well strip down to jib and engine – particularly when the destination is right in the eye of the wind, and a flat storm jib and engine will narrow the tacks. Short-tacking in a narrow channel once safety is reached is best done with the engine turning the boat through the wind to make absolutely sure that there is no humiliating grounding in sight of the yacht club bar, or mere yards from a berth or mooring.

Tactical running

Contemporary yachts are not rigged for running before the wind in the same way as traditional sailing craft fitted with square-sails, so that the spinnaker has become the down-wind substitute. However, except in racing craft, the spinnaker is a light-weather sail, set from turtles and muzzled by squeezers and snuffers, so that when rough weather compels low sails they tend to be fore-and-aft sails – canvas acting in its least efficient mode and in the wrong plane. One method of getting the best out of these sails is to parallel the up-wind tacking technique with a down-wind equivalent, and this entails frequent gybes.

The sequence of events making up a gybe centres on easing the main boom from one side of the boat to the other without risk of damage or injury. First, the preventer is taken off and brought round for use on the other down-wind tack. Then the mainsheet is brought in slowly and secured. The order "gybe-ho" is given, and the helmsman puts the helm up so that the stern comes to wind. The tethered boom quivers, the sail flaps, and the gear jerks over with the wind now on its other side. The mainsheet crewman does *not* uncleat and let the rope slide through his hands, for that way lies rope-burn, but pays out the sheet hand-over-hand until the boom is far enough out to let the sail draw properly. The headsail sheets will have been handled in a similar manner as with an up-wind tack, for after "gybe-ho" and the collapse of the "old" sail the "old" sheet is first eased out and then let fly as the "new" sheet is winched home. When both sails are drawing nicely, the preventer goes back on the boom.

Down-wind steering

Helmsmanship down-wind needs, if anything, more concentration than steering up-wind, for corrections have to be made *before* the bow has swung on the lift of a wave. These corrections must be both rapid and small, and the man at the helm should remember that after about 20° of rudder has been applied its action is more in the nature of a brake than a steering device. When steering and slewed round by a particularly nasty sea the tendency is to put on full correcting rudder, but it must be resisted as counter-productive because once you get into a see-saw of this kind it takes ages to steady the boat down again. My technique when running in a rolling sea is to be slightly off-square as the crest of the next wave reaches the stern, then "flick" the wheel to get a 90° angle to the crest and ride over the top at full power. The idea is that speed is maintained into the trough, and as the boat passes through the trough it can again go slightly off-square to catch a ride on the next wave. The helmsman is the one person on board to know when a boat is being pressed too hard, and this moment often coincides with a call for tiller lines, lashings or a tackle to hold her on course. Once there is an appreciation that wind and sea are dominating performance the time arises for a new initiative, and this initiative can take one of seven forms. They are: shortening sail, scudding, heaving-to, "dodging", bare poles, lying-to and lying a-hull.

Shortening sail and scudding

The illustrations in Chapter Four suggested what combinations of sail may be carried in specific wind strengths, but in no case was a vessel shown with a single sail. Fig. 36 has a boat jogging along under trysail alone, and the corollary is the deployment of a single headsail. An example comes to mind. The late Adlard Coles said that ". . . if the sea is really rough, the average small yacht cannot make progress beating to windward against a strong foul spring tide off a headland". (I take this quote from p. 59 of *Heavy Weather Sailing*, that splendid classic by Adlard Coles. First published in 1967, it is currently being revised by Alan Green of the Royal Ocean Racing Club with a view to re-issue.)

The situation described by Adlard Coles appears in Fig. 41. A yacht has battled its way to a point between Black Head and Lizard Head, having had the original intention of getting round to Penzance. The skipper has noted the adverse combination of wind, tide and headland and has modified his plan by turning away with the wind on the quarter to scud for Falmouth. Scudding used to mean running with studding sails set, but the term is now used to describe running with the wind abaft the beam and a smooth and easy motion – just the ticket for the crew of a yacht that have taken down the main, given up working to windward and have a fair prospect of "all night in".

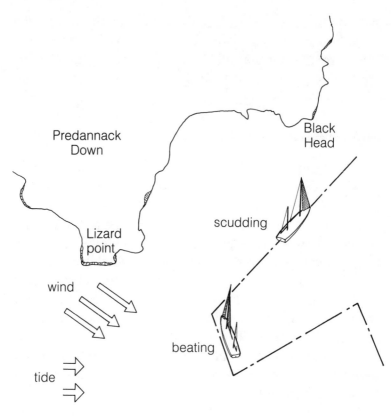

Fig. 41   Scudding

Heaving-to

We have already discussed what to do; now for when to do it. Naturally, the moment to go about and back the headsail is when there is a "smooth", and that moment must be well before it becomes dangerous to make the turn. Heave-to early, hardening in the mainsheet or trysail sheet as you go round and letting the boat settle before lashing the wheel or tiller in the down-helm position. The amount of water coming on board will reduce to occasional splashes, and although the hull will rise and fall it tends to remain at a liveable angle. With plenty of sea room and no shipping about the crew can get below, dry out, eat and drink and take some rest. If the weather improves, it is possible to get the best of both worlds by unlashing the helm and progressively slackening the headsail sheet to achieve the fore-reaching position and, ultimately, go back on the original course.

Dodging

Dodging is a tactic much used by trawlers, and consists of motoring slowly into the wind at about 2 or 3 knots and keeping that wind precisely on the bow. Motorsailers and boats with high, flared bows will have the greatest success and, of course, you will need to watch fuel consumption. It is ideal for craft with a wheelhouse or dual steering position in the saloon/deckhouse because they are built with a view to taking seas over the bow and the helmsman and lookout are reasonably certain to stay warm and dry.

Bare poles

This method takes us slightly beyond the brief of this book as the first of three rather desperate remedies, but the theory is that when the wind gets too strong and all sails are down the masts act as sails and the boat can be steered down-wind. It seems, by all accounts, that about 50 knots of wind is needed before bare poles is a feasible solution, and as this is Force 10 on the Beaufort Scale we can pass on to lying-to, which is a sensible proposition for small craft caught out in winds beyond their usual experience.

Lying-to

Originally, the procedure adopted was to stream a hooped canvas sea-anchor over the bows to keep the boat's head roughly to the wind and sea, and use of the method owed much to the writings of Captain Voss, a Victorian adventurer who made some spectacular voyages in a converted dug-out canoe. A heavy duty drogue on the same pattern is still used by Royal National Lifeboat Institution craft, and sleeve drogues, perforated drogues, series drogues and parachute drogues have all been developed in recent years. The method has changed, however, because while lying-to with a sea-anchor over the bow often results in taking the seas on the beam rather than the bow, putting the same equipment over the stern while running has had some notably good results. After successively reducing sail to a storm jib and scudding down-wind, it is helpful to put long warps, or a drogue, over the stern to slow the boat down, prevent a broach and assist steering. When the last sail comes down, the craft is lying-to its drogue, still by the stern.

Small craft with the early need to face rough seas rarely carry sea-anchors or drogues, and two methods of improvisation are depicted in Fig. 42. The craft at the top started running down-wind under a headsail, and then put some long warps in the water to assist steering. When the sail was dowsed the resourceful crew added a "drag" of two motor tyres on warps to act as a sea-anchor. The crew of the yacht shown at the foot of Fig. 42 had a windage problem, and when they removed the boom and its sail altogether to cut down windage it was fastened to a warp and chain and put off over the bow to serve as a head-to-wind drogue and to break the advancing seas.

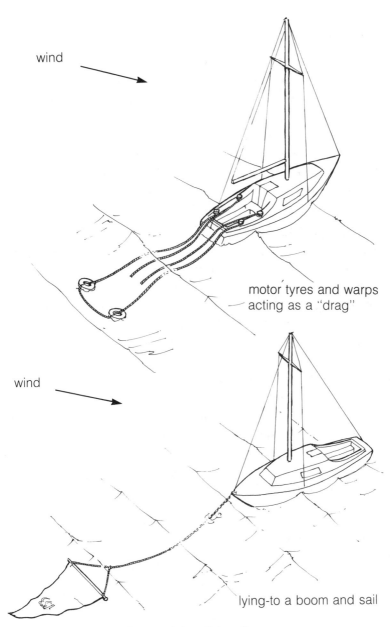

wind

motor tyres and warps
acting as a "drag"

wind

lying-to a boom and sail

Fig. 42   Lying-to. Improvising "drag"

Lying a-hull

Grounded in the old Lancashire (or is it Yorkshire?) saying that goes "when in doubt, do nowt!", the basis of lying a-hull is that the crew drops and secures all sail, lashes the helm alee and goes below, firmly closing the hatch behind them. Of course the tactic relies very heavily on having "sea roome enough" and on there being no big ships about, but is often adopted when crew morale is low; cold, seasickness and weariness have taken over, and darkness, fog or heavy rain make the cockpit the least desirable spot on board. The yacht will tend to lie beam on to the seas so that the rolling may be frightful, and the obligation to keep a lookout and work the pumps remains. As a general rule, people will not want to get into their bunks when lying a-hull, and the usual thing is to put all the cushions, mattresses and sleeping bags down on the cabin sole so that sleepers finish up like the meat part of a sausage toad, all embedded in a soft batter of textiles.

The experience of the ages is that boats survive while humans crack, and lying a-hull, uncomfortable and morale-depressing as it is, may be justified on two grounds. It seems to be the tactic which results in least damage to boats caught out in stormy weather, and it is the easiest manoeuvre that a hard-pressed vessel can perform.

Harbour cares

Statistics show that most hull damage takes place in harbour. As this is the most expensive type of damage to repair it will do no harm to end this chapter with some do's and don'ts on reaching shelter.

Coming in to anchor in hard winds, remember that

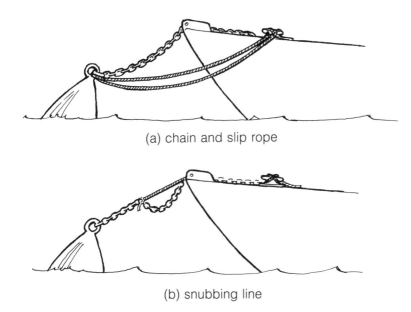

(a) chain and slip rope

(b) snubbing line

Fig. 43   Harbour care

you should allow for *five* times the depth of water when paying out anchor chain rather than the usual three-and-a-bit, and that the anchor will hold better if you motor it in by going astern after it engages the bottom. When taking up a mooring, attach the anchor chain *and* a slip rope, as in the top half of Fig. 43. Later, if the grinding of chain or the snubbing of the slip rope disturbs your rest, it is best to fit a snubbing line (lower part of Fig. 43) that will keep the noise and jerk to a minimum. When entering a crowded port where you have to lie alongside another yacht, follow the practice outlined in Fig. 44 and lie head to tail so that the two sets of crosstrees do not clout each other. Note also in Fig. 44 that the outboard yacht has carried its head and stern lines to the quay so that the cleats of the inboard vessel do not have to bear excessive wrenching strains. Finally, if detained in port

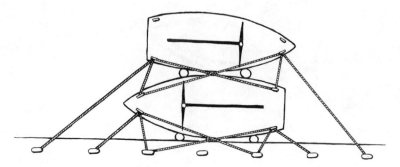

Fig. 44 Yachts moored head and tail

for several days think about chafe. "Freshen the nips" in your lines by altering the points of contact daily, and put plastic tubing where the warps are likely to rub, particularly in the fairleads. So that the plastic tubing does not wander down the warp and become ineffective, bore a hole at one end and secure the tubing to the warp with a piece of cord. For the rest, it is a question of weather-watching, patience, courteous behaviour to those next door and waiting for the next forecast.

Chapter Seven
REPEATING THE DOSE

"Send your patient at once into the coolest place that you can find, get his head shaved, apply cold to it, and give an ounce of castor oil immediately, repeating the dose until the bowels are freely and thoroughly voided four or five times."

Instructions for dealing with cases of sunstroke in the Ship Captain's Medical Guide *of 1868*

First aid is all about damage limitation, and what is suggested in this chapter is in no way a substitute for skilled medical attention but merely sketches out those sensible steps that stop bad becoming worse. I begin with heatstroke; not because it is a major problem in windy northern waters but because the remedies are pure damage limitation and demonstrate perfectly the essentials of first aid. Incidentally, the quotation with which this chapter began illustrates the *wrong* way of imparting information to amateur medicos because it goes beyond minimising the consequences of illness and attempts a somewhat bizarre course of treatment. That, no doubt, was the correct approach in 1868 when ships might be weeks or months from a port with hospitals; it does not apply today.

Heatstroke

Heatstroke is signalled by sudden unconsciousness or collapse, with the sufferer having a hot and dry skin and a high temperature. Undress him or her completely – this is no time for modesty – and wrap the patient's whole body in sheets or towels soaked in cold water. Renew at intervals until the temperature has fallen from about 107°F to 102°F or lower.

The lesser condition of heat collapse, or sunstroke, shows itself in general weakness, headache, dizziness, vomiting and a cold sweat. The treatment is to put victims in a cool place, such as the shaded part of the foredeck where wind blows down the headsail, give them plenty of water with added salt in it to drink, and pour a bucket of sea water over them. Motor to windward if you want to get the maximum cooling breeze.

In both cases look at the urine produced after some hours of fairly constant absorption. If it is clear, things are on the mend. If cloudy, or green, keep the cooling and wetting process going.

Burns and scalds

Burns and scalds are probably the commonest types of rough weather injuries, being occasioned by rope friction, chemicals, boiling liquid or flames and in all such cases the major problem is sepsis. At one time it was thought that this type of wound should be merely covered with a sterile dressing and left alone, but current thinking is that cold water be applied for at least ten minutes. Similarly, it was once anathema to prick blisters; now it is recommended.

In the case of chemical burns, usually from acids, it is best to first wash the effected part with cold water and then with diluted bicarbonate of soda. Afterwards, dab dry with cotton wool, and cover lightly with a sterile dressing. Cold, salt water is perfectly all right for external application; a severe burn or scald leads to fluid loss so that the fresh water liquid intake should be doubled for 24 hours.

Savlon is good for a healing burn or scald, and when a blister is as full as it is going to be it can be pricked with the point of a safety pin that has been sterilized in a flame or boiling water, but *not* pressed.

Choking

When a large object such as false teeth or unchewed food lodges in the throat there is the danger of death by asphyxia. The first aid response is to expel the object by a sudden rush of air up the windpipe.

In the left-hand part of Fig. 45 the patient has been slung over the knees of a seated companion and is being thumped between the shoulder blades with quick, hard blows. Should he be lying face upwards, kneel astride

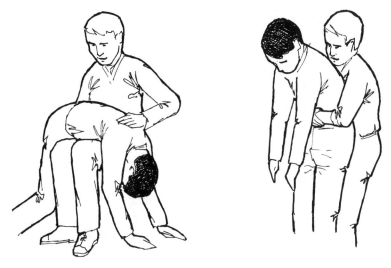

Fig. 45 Blow between shoulder blades and Heimlich's Hug

and put the heel of the hand in the upper belly, place the other hand on top of it and thrust vigorously, repeating at measured intervals.

Once the obstruction is cleared, put the patient in the coma position (Fig. 47) to keep the airways clear. A victim who is able to stand can be given Heimlich's Hug – as in the right-hand part of Fig. 45. Stand behind the patient with your clenched fist in the upper belly below the front of the rib cage. Put your other hand over the clenched fist and give a sudden violent hug, continuing in a lifting, thrusting movement until the blocking material shoots out of the throat. When it is all over put the patient in the coma position to recover.

Teeth

Having mentioned false teeth, this is a good moment to deal with a greatly-neglected area of first aid. Dental injuries are more common than you might think – particularly as many yachtsman are living in that long valley between fifty and sixty years of age – so that not only are living teeth broken by flailing shackles and swinging blocks, but crowns, bridges and fillings get damaged in the rough and tumble of a day at sea. The solution is to carry a Dentanurse kit which contains the means of giving first aid to damaged gums, pulp or nerves, and of making temporary repairs to crowns and bridges plus the insertion of temporary fillings. Toothache is a great morale-lowerer, and the pain may be lessened by rubbing the gums in the area of the aching tooth with neat rum, while a hollow tooth that is giving trouble should be filled with the same liquid, using an eye dropper for the purpose.

Hypothermia and resuscitation

Following man overboard and the recovery of him from the sea in an unconscious state, the first question that arises is which comes next – resuscitation or reversing the effects of hypothermia? In severe hypothermia the heart beat is so feeble that it may barely be detected; heart massage may cause ventricular fibrillation and death, and it is worth remembering that in northern waters most people who die following prolonged immersion do so from hypothermia rather than drowning. If the body feels ice-cold a rapid re-warm by a space blanket, sleeping bags, wool blankets or non-contact hot water bottles is a must. Recuscitation can then begin. You should make a mental note, therefore, that although Fig. 46 and Fig. 47 show the subject unclothed the reality is that he will invariably be buried under a mass of warming material while resuscitation takes place. The process has three stages.

In Fig. 46(a) the patient has been put on his back, his mouth cleared of any obstructions and his forehead pressed back. Keep this position, pinch his nose to close the nostrils and place your mouth over his – as in 46(b) – to make a good seal. Blow, giving six quick inflations

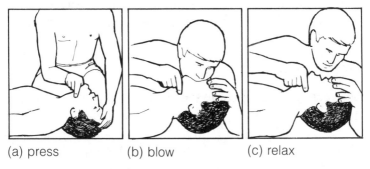

(a) press   (b) blow   (c) relax

Fig. 46   Resuscitation

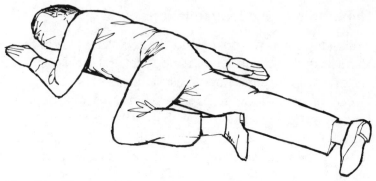

Fig. 47   The coma (or recovery) position

followed by deep, slow ones of about five seconds' dura-
tion. If, after one minute, his colour has not changed
from blue-grey to pink and his chest is not rising and
falling of its own accord, strike the breastbone sharply
with your fist. Make it a good thump, because broken
ribs are an acceptable alternative to a lost life. Should
your efforts be successful and the victim begins breathing
steadily he should be placed in the recovery, or coma,
position shown in Fig. 47, but still warmly covered and
his mouth and nose clear of anything that could cause
suffocation. If this procedure has not worked on the first
attempt, KEEP TRYING FOR AT LEAST AN HOUR.
Repeat the whole cycle, using a Brook airway from the
first aid kit and a relay of breathers for the purpose.

Signs of life

Between wars few people see dead bodies, and if resuscitation apparently fails, or hypothermia seems to triumph,
you cannot rely on the conventional condensing of breath
on a mirror or ear to the chest to make sure that it is all
over. In particular, I recall one occasion when a crewman,

long disabled by seasickness, gave all the appearances of death with virtually no vital signs at all. However, by trying the three tests set out below we were able to confirm that he was in one of those comatose states where the body has reduced all activity to a minimum and is, literally, shamming death. As you may be guessing, he recovered once the boat was safely tied to a pontoon. The three infallible tests for life are:

1. A pulse in the artery deep below the angle of the jawbone.
2. The skin blanches under the pressure of a forefinger, and then becomes pink again when the finger is removed.
3. The pupils of the eye alter in size when a light is shone into them.

Shock

After hypothermia, shock is the major killer. It is a state of collapse that may complicate either a serious injury, exposure or a minor cutting or crushing episode that of itself does not endanger life. Signs are rapid and weak breathing, cold and clammy limbs and a weak or irregular pulse. The remedy is warmth and rest of the lying-down kind, and if the sufferer is very pale and tends to be irritable or irrational it is a good idea to raise the legs so as to restore blood to the upper part of the body in general and the brain in particular. Reassurance may be needed, and if the shock is so severe as to lead to a total blackout place the patient in the coma position depicted in Fig. 47.

One problem that arises when delayed shock occurs in someone who has "bottled-up" reaction to an incident is recognising the linkage after a lapse of time and making the right connection, for it is all too easy to see shock as something new rather than relating it to what went before. No alcohol, of course, but sips of fluid and a calm listening demeanour will work best.

Cuts and wounds

First, remove any large foreign body from the wound and press a sterile pad onto it for at least ten minutes. Press hard, and do not take it off at any time. If the pad gets soaked with blood add another on top. Do *NOT* take it off to look at the wound at this stage. When the patient is lying down it may be possible to lift the wounded limb or portion of torso to make the heart's pumping action harder and slow the amount of blood getting to the gash. If the wound is long and deep do nothing more than bandage the pad or pads in place and leave the rest for skilled attention ashore. Small cuts that have ceased to ooze blood may be cleaned up with soapy water, making sure that the swabbing motions are away from the wound itself. In years gone by these cuts were then secured and covered with adhesive tape, but the ideal covering now-

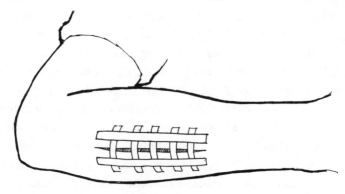

Fig. 48   Ladder pattern of closures

adays is butterfly strips (Steristrips) that are half adhesive plaster and half stitches that hold the edges together wonderfully well. These closures will also cope with quite large wounds when used in ladder pattern, as shown in Fig. 48, and this is a far better technique than trying to sew wounds together in a seaway with consequent risk of sepsis and a disfiguring result.

Fractures

A break in a bone is telegraphed by pain and tenderness which is much increased when an attempt is made to move that part of the body. The first-aider's prime duty is to do no more damage, and for that reason he should not so lash the limb that circulation is lost.

Usually, it is possible to lash one part of the body to another – finger to finger, leg to leg or arm to body – and inflatable splints can be put in place to surround and support the limb before inflation to induce immobility. If you need something larger try sail battens, which are tough yet have some "give" in them, or even a padded ensign staff for a leg fracture. The general principle when splinting is to immobilise the joint above and the joint below the break, and to move the injured limb as little as possible. Should the fingers or toes turn blue or white you must release the splints and bandages immediately to restore circulation, and when refastening do so at lesser pressure.

One type of injury common in rough weather is the fracture of the collar-bone. This is a defence injury often caused by putting out an arm to break a fall, with the result that the impact is carried up that arm and snaps the bone. Typically, the casualty will get up supporting the elbow on the injured side, inclining his head in that

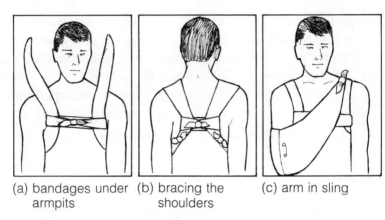

(a) bandages under   (b) bracing the   (c) arm in sling
    armpits   shoulders

Fig. 49   Bandaging a broken collar-bone

direction and "hugging" the arm. Five bandages will be
needed to secure a broken collar-bone until skilled attention may be obtained, and the order of work appears in
Fig. 49. Support the arm on the injured side and pass
triangular folded bandages under both armpits, knotting
them at the back. To stop them slipping, put a third
conforming bandage across the breast – as in Fig.
49(a). At the back, secure both the loops with a fourth
bandage which braces the shoulders back – Fig. 49(b)
– and corrects the tendency of the broken ends of the
collar bone to grate painfully together. Finally, support
the elbow on the injured side by putting the arm in a
sling made from a triangular bandage, as in Fig. 49(c),
and get the injured person wedged into a corner of the
cabin with his sound side against the structure and the
painful part facing outwards.

Embedded fish hooks

There are two schools of thought on this subject: one that
believes fish hooks should come out the way they went

in; and the push-through-and-cut-off adherents. I go along with the latter, and Fig. 50 has the basics of removing hooks. With a pair of pliers, push the hook in such a way as to get its tip back out through the skin sufficiently far to cut the barb off. Then withdraw the

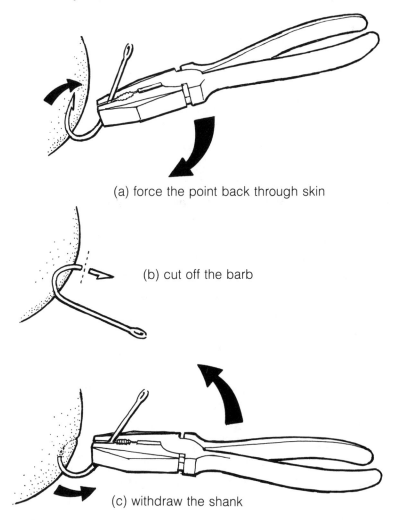

(a) force the point back through skin

(b) cut off the barb

(c) withdraw the shank

Fig. 50   Removal of fish hook

remainder of the shank back the way it went in, as in the third part of Fig. 50. It is less painful if the push through and withdrawal are done quickly, and if there are no other means of deadening pain in the case of a fish hook in a finger it is best to dangle the hand over the side or in a bucket of cold sea water to "freeze" the area temporarily. Fish hooks are usually most unsterile, having been coated at various times in rotting bait and fish guts, so that a follow-up course of antibiotics will invariably be needed.

Stings and boils

It is the trivial things of life that often cause the most trouble, and insect stings can be maddening while jellyfish stings cause maximum discomfort and desperate scratching. In the latter case, try Avomine which is more usually taken for travel sickness but has a lot of anti-histamine in it and will soothe the hurt. Insect stings may be countered with anti-histamine creams or calamine cream and ointment. Boils often occur at awkward places, like at the neck where an oilskin rubs, and if not treated they tend to spread. Boils are best managed by bringing them to a head with moist heat and then, when they "point" and are fully ready for it, lance them and drain the crater. Wrap a metal spoon in a cloth and put it in boiling water. Bring the spoon and steaming cloth as close to the boil as may be, being guided by the sufferer's reaction if you get too close. Do not hurry the process, and have several stabs at bringing the boil "out" before thinking of lancing it as premature penetration may spread the infection. After lancing, do not cover the area but keep it dry, wiping it occasionally with a dilute antiseptic and letting the air get to it.

First aid box contents

Most first aid boxes made for sale as a commercial proposition either contain too much of the manufacturer's own brand of products (quite often bandages or plasters), or have a restricted range of medicaments and hardware only suitable for industrial or motor vehicle accident purposes. The boxes themselves are of hinged metal: for boat use you need air-tight plastic containers like those sold originally with large quantities of ice cream in them. In any case, it will be necessary to make up your own list of contents, and some suggestions follow. In the first paragraph appear the "hard" contents; in the second the drugs, ointments and medicines. (The Dentanurse kit previously mentioned is extra to these requirements.)

Dressings, bandages and hardware

4 triangular bandages
3 conforming bandages
2 15g sterile cotton wool
  packs
3 large wound dressings
3 medium wound
  dressings
1 pack of sterile
  non-adhesive dressings
1 packet of burn
  dressings
1 roll of stretch fabric
  dressing strip

1 tin band aids/
  Elastoplast
1 pair of sharp scissors
8 non-rusting safety pins
1 thermometer
1 packet Steristrips
1 eye dropper
2 finger stalls
1 pair tweezers
1 space blanket
1 Brook airway
1 Eye dropper

Drugs, ointments and medicines

1 packet Paracetamol
tablets

1 packet Avomine,
Hyoscine or Stugeron
tablets for seasickness
sufferers

1 bottle Piriton tablets for
bites and stings

1 bottle Fortral tablets for
use as a heavy duty pain
killer

1 bottle Dettol

1 mini-bottle of Locorten
Vioform ear drops

2 tubes Savlon

1 jar Vaseline

1 bottle Amoxil tablets for
antibiotic purposes

1 tube Bayolin for muscular
or rheumatic pains

1 10ml mini-bottle of
Hypromellose eye drops

1 bottle calamine lotion

Index

BY THE SAME AUTHOR
Order Form on next page

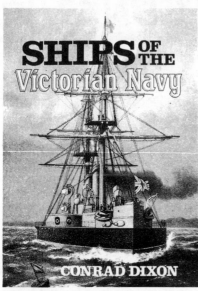

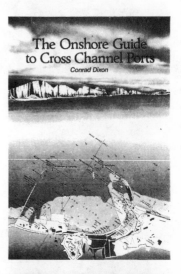

Ships of the Victorian Navy
Text by Conrad Dixon
Illustrations from the original editions of 1872 and 1881
This book illustrates the important period of transition from wooden sailing ships to steel ships driven by turbines. Each ship is described in detail and accompanied by a full page 19th Century full colour stone litho illustration by the renowned maritime artist Fred Mitchell.
112 pages 48 full colour illustrations
HB £14.95   1 85253 033 2
PB £8.95   1 85253 024 3

The Onshore Guide to Cross Channel Ports
Conrad Dixon
Takes up where the cruising handbooks leave you. The coast is dealt with in sections so that intermediate ports, minor havens and anchorages are grouped with the featured ports that have full treatment. The facilities are presented alphabetically with a symbol for each facility and showing its position on the map. Addresses and telephone numbers are given for most of the vital services, and some of the merely useful.
PB 148 pages 31 maps
£7.50   1 85253 068 5

Grounding, Stranding and Wreck
Conrad Dixon
This is a book which no skipper should be without. Written by a man of proven experience its primary purpose is to set the reader on the right train of thought when a stranding takes place. What is done, or not done in the first five minutes makes all the difference between minor setback and major disaster.
PB 120 pages 20 illustrations
£6.50   1 85253 075 8

MORE TITLES FROM ASHFORD
Available from Chandleries, Booksellers or by post

The Boatbuilding Book Geoffrey O'Connell How to fit out a glass fibre shell.	£15.95	....
The Boat Owner's Maintenance Book Geoffrey O'Connell Keeps maintenance as painless as possible.	£15.95	....
Canvas Work Jeremy Howard-Williams Simple and advanced projects for boat, home and garden.	£6.95	....
Emergency Navigation David Burch Steering by stars, sun or even clouds when more modern methods fail!	£16.95	....
Grounding, Stranding and Wreck Conrad Dixon No skipper should be without it.	£6.50	....
Log of Christopher Columbus Robert Fuson Translation of the famous log. Reads like an adventure story.	£16.95	....
Marine Diesel Engines Nigel Calder Maintenance, troubleshooting and repair.	£14.95	....
The Onshore Guide to Cross Channel Ports Conrad Dixon Takes up where cruising handbooks leave off.	£7.50	....
Ships of the Victorian Navy Conrad Dixon Full details spanning wooden sailing ships to turbine driven steel.	£14.95 (hb).... £8.95 (pb)....	

If you have difficulty obtaining any of these books, they are available direct from Ashford. Please add 10% to cover p&p.

This is only a small selection of our titles. Please tick box for our free catalogue for more information about books on a wide range of nautical subjects. □

Name   . . . .

Address   . . . .

. . . .

TOTAL	£
(add 10% p&p)	£
Cheque **enclosed**	£

**Or debit my Access/Visa/
American Express Card No**

Expiry Date . . . .

Ashford, 1 Church Road, Shedfield, Hants SO3 2HW   Tel. No. 0329 834265